GOD'S UNFINISHED BUSINESS

GOD'S UNFINISHED BUSINESS
Evolution of humanity

John Wilding & Margaret Boaden

Janus Publishing Company
London, England

First Published in Great Britain 2005 by
Janus Publishing Company Ltd,
105-107 Gloucester Place,
London W1U 6BY

www.januspublishing.co.uk

Copyright © 2005 by John Wilding & Margaret Boaden
The authors have asserted their moral rights

British Library Cataloguing-in-Publication Data
A catalogue record for this book
is available from the British Library

ISBN 1 85756 641 6

Cover design: Hannah Lewis

Printed and bound in Great Britain

"The authors are grateful to Mike Smith and Paul Wilding who read earlier versions of this book and made many invaluable suggestions. We hope we have done justice to their insightful comments."

For further information and opportunity to comment, please visit the authors' website at www.humanfuture.co.uk

Contents

Prologue	i
The Search	1
The World We Live In	11
A Different Approach	31
Jesus' God and His Purpose	71
The Authority of Jesus	99
Creation	119
Coming to the End of the Religious Set-up	135
References	143
Index	149

Prologue

This book is intended for readers who are dissatisfied equally with the materialistic certainties of much contemporary science, the competitive self-interest of the current political and economic scene and the divisive dogmatism characteristic of religions. It is for those who are looking for a practical and realistic view of the purpose of life, consistent with modern knowledge, that can be relevant to the whole of humanity and replace restless striving for individual pleasure.

Religious allegiance, plus political and economic ambition, threatens to become, as in the past, one of the divisive forces of our time. Conversely, many blame the decline in religious adherence in Britain for weakening the forces that held together families and communities, encouraged concern for others and respect for authority. So is religion a force for ill or a force for good, or both?

A dispassionate view of history suggests that religion unites in order to divide. Religions have arisen within "tribes" in order to enlist supernatural forces against rivals. So religions are essentially self-regarding in their purpose, whether as a rallying force for society, or in reassuring the individual of personal salvation in this life or the next. They are one facet of the competitive struggle to do better than others. They promise that making the right bargain with the god and performing the proper sacrifice will create a favoured people. They lay down rules about the proper performance of rituals, the required style of hair, dress and food, the role of special intermediaries, all designed to set the faithful apart from the unfavoured. All this is divisive.

Christians will argue that their religion is not like that, but is driven by love for others, not by competition with others, but it often bears all the hallmarks identified above. Christians will also claim that no sacrifice or ritual is needed to keep the Christian God on side, but in lieu of this we have a bizarre doctrine of a god who had to be appeased by the death of his Son, which is even less flattering to the deity, and which comes out of St Paul's inability to shed his Jewish past. As for the need to keep rules, it lies close to the surface of many worshippers' understanding of their faith.

All this bears little relation to the teaching of the "founder" (quotation marks, because surely Jesus never intended to launch such a system). His teaching suggests something quite different, a plea for human beings to take a further "evolutionary" step beyond the competition of the "selfish gene" to a better mode of living. Jesus said we must be "born again" to see things differently from the usual self-interested viewpoint and become like the God he depicted rather than inventing human-like gods to serve our selfish interests. This God, he argued, did not have a list of rules to be followed, did not punish "sinners", did not require special rites of worship and did not exercise power in the way human beings operate. On the contrary, the great underlying principle of the universe was love, putting others first, working together (as, it may be noted, the supposedly selfish genes have to do) rather than in competition with each other. Being born again has nothing to do with a warm glow of self-satisfaction, but requires radical changes at both the personal and the corporate level in priorities in relation to economics, the environment, regard for the truth, systems of justice, exercise of power and relations with each other. It is time, this book argues, for humanity to abandon the competition which currently drives human life and embark upon a worthy celebration of the life and death of this visionary, more worthy of him than the quarrels that have marked Christian history. Such a step might also ensure that humans do not destroy the world, and it would certainly mean the death of divisive religion and its trappings.

Chapter 1
The Search

There's something different about Glastonbury. Most towns in England now look almost identical, the same shops in the high street, the same signs to the car park, the shopping mall, the public conveniences, the nearest motorway. But in Glastonbury hardly a single shop offers just the conventional. There's no obvious burger bar, though no doubt there is one somewhere. There are the massive remains of the Abbey, once a focal point of Christianity in this out-of-the-way corner of England, destroyed in a king's personal power struggle which intertwined the political and the religious issues. But most prominent on every side are the offers and claims of an alternative lifestyle which promises the self-fulfilment that many feel that capitalist materialism has failed to deliver.

The biggest bookshop in the town is a dazzling array of clamouring claims to reveal the truth, self-authenticated golden paths to fulfilment, the secret of life, physical and mental health beyond our dreams, and above all personal peace and happiness. For an academic scientist long accustomed to a spirit of continuous proposing and disproving of hypotheses and careful experimental tests against reality, together with the need to consider the healthy scepticism of others, these brash claims of a mass of bright book jackets are bewildering, and provoke scorn and rejection. Certainly they cannot all be true. Have any of them been properly tested? Who buys all these outpourings? Who believes them in an age where rational science and technology supposedly rule our lives and control our world? But they must be quite profitable. Most of us receive, from time to time, "unbeatable offers" to revolutionise our lives, increase our creativity, solve all health problems. Recent personal experiences include offers to show how "Eastern principles can help us to think and act in a way that brings good fortune and fulfilment" or how to "use magic to rid your home of bad spirits or mend a broken heart", the offer of a rose quartz pendant which "allows us to release our fears and cleanse ourselves of anger" (would that it were that easy!) and an advertisement for cards which contain "angelic messages [that] focus on the key areas of love, wisdom, healing, career and creativity".

This is one of the paradoxes of human thinking, particularly in our westernised culture. Questions about the meaning of life may seem largely buried beneath issues of everyday living like the price of petrol and proposed taxation levels. The main focus seems to be on how to get more of the "good things" of life, and to get them quickly, an approach consciously, or perhaps unconsciously, based on the belief that the good life amounts to nothing more than these things and that there is nothing beyond this physical existence on earth. For science has demonstrated (so we are told) that the whole universe and the emergence of life and thinking human beings are no more than the outcome of a gigantic lottery, so we may as well enjoy what the dice bring to us here and now, taking advantage of our growing ability to control the physical world, and exploit its riches for our own short-term benefit.

So one moment we humans are confident we can do almost anything – fly to the moon, walk on the seabed, you name it, we can do it. But this confidence is fragile, for the next moment we are so unsure of ourselves that we behave more like a child who needs teacher to help button a coat. One moment we are ready to defy anybody and anything to assert our individuality and creativity. The next moment we are terrified of anybody who steps out of line and look for ways to constrain such a person. One moment we perform prodigious feats of transporting spare organs half way across the globe to save one person's life. The next we helplessly shrug our shoulders at the death of millions from starvation or disease. One moment we can be ravished by the beauty of the human body or the

The Search

natural world or some creation of human imagination, the next we can protect our insecurity by closing our minds to the prospect of devastation more dreadful than the ancients' dreams of hell. One moment sublime, the next ridiculous or appalling.

These deeper insecurities which lie just below the surface of modern life, even in affluent societies, can suddenly emerge when disaster strikes, as after the death of Princess Diana in Britain or the destruction of the twin towers in New York. Suddenly a spasm of emotion gripped the nations. Like children unexpectedly frightened by the prospect of being left alone in a strange place, adults sought to cling to nurse, often in the form of the churches which they probably ignored normally, for reassurance that someone was keeping an eye on them and on the threatening world around them to keep it under control. Religion is expected to be there when reassurance and a safety net are needed, whether it is to support us in our weakness or to host important ceremonies of life in a suitably dignified way (birth, marriage, death or state occasions, particularly ones with military associations). The rest of the time we can manage by ourselves, thank you, because most of that stuff is childish and unbelievable, or makes excessive demands on our valuable time and money.

These insecurities are likely to have been one of the original driving forces from which religions emerged, and they continue to trigger similar responses even in our more sceptical culture. One response is the survival of the primitive urge of our ancestors when confronted with forces they could not control, to try to establish a bargain with the gods whom they believed did control these forces. The worshippers carry out appropriate rituals and sacrifices to the gods and hope that in return the gods will look after their own, control the forces of nature, ensure that the new seeds germinate and grow. Yet gods who need or can be persuaded by such practices offer feeble grounds for confidence. Another underlying theme of religion is that those who make the right bargain and stick to it are a special people, favoured by the gods, and all others are inferior. In consequence, rigid regimes are prescribed for the faithful (often by men for women and children). There is no concern for all humanity.

Such attitudes are, of course, intertwined with a whole host of other judgements about what and who is acceptable to the gods and to the group concerned. Such attitudes lead to divisions between people and have been used to justify innumerable horrors by one group against another, not least by Christians. A third theme of religion is that truth is the preserve of the religion, laid out in tradition or a sacred text and immutable. Set forms of worship are prescribed or some specific way of achieving a purer, superior way of life. Thus in their origins religions have the same aims as the rest of human behaviour, and gods have been created to serve the immediate perceived needs of some human group, even or particularly when in conflict with other groups. Such basically selfish purposes are present still in the supposedly more sophisticated "higher" religions, even when transmuted into the longer-term aim of gaining a reward beyond this life.

As examples of this limited and "selfish" focus that tends to characterise religions, we need look no further than some of the most influential religions in the world today. Islam promises paradise for those who keep the rules laid down in the Koran. Judaism holds fast to the claim that the Jews are a special people chosen of God, and, despite their experience over the centuries, still believes that they are entirely correct in pursuing the fulfilment of the promises spelt out in the Old Testament, which justify turning others off the land once promised to the Jewish people. Buddhism offers a way to get to a point of individual development that removes the demands of the physical, by following hundreds of rules. Christianity typically makes similar promises of personal fulfilment. For example, the Alpha course (widely used in recent years to introduce Christianity to new enquirers) focusses on the message that Jesus came to redeem humanity from sin, and if you accept this then your place in heaven is assured. To quote a recent critic, "Alpha was all about what Christianity could do for Me, Me, Me" (Mike Purton, *The Guardian*, 1 December 2001).

We argue here, however, that all these appeals to self-interest are a dead end, leading nowhere and at worst to oblivion, since they create discord, disharmony and dissatisfaction. So religions are not only challenged by the scientific demonstrations of the origins and nature of the universe and of life, but they have a weak claim to provide a higher purpose, a counterweight to the competitive struggle which is supposedly the inevitable consequence of the way that creation has evolved. On the contrary, they are themselves an outcome of that same process, born of the drive to control and compete. They are a source of divisions, intolerance and prejudice which damage humanity's efforts, weak though these may be, to mitigate the worst features of the struggle for survival.

Faced with the failures of formal religions to provide satisfaction for the yearnings for spiritual comfort and reassurance, many have turned to the more exotic promises typified in the Glastonbury bookshops. Again, such promises are, above all, individualistic, offering escape rather than a hope that is relevant to the state of the world that we see illustrated daily in the media. We are in a world of inequality, misery for many alongside ridiculous wealth for some, growing destruction of the basic resources on which all life depends, violence and insecurity. Surely, if there is some higher reality in which life is meant to be more than competition for possessions with the weakest going to the wall, promises of fulfilment should first and foremost address the mess the world is in and offer a way to change it, not just the comfort of separate individuals. On the other hand, if there is no reality beyond the physical world we experience, the best we can do is to mitigate the suffering of others, moved by compassion or perhaps by the wish to prevent their turning against us and destroying our comforts. Or we can simply ignore them, on the grounds that none of this has any ultimate significance.

And so, the dilemmas which face those who seek a more fulfilling life for all than is currently possible may be summarised as follows:

1. Science claims to explain the origin of the universe, the development of life forms and eventually of human beings as having involved no more than the arrangement and rearrangement of matter into particular patterns, a process due to chance plus survival of the patterns which possessed the more "useful" qualities.

2. If this is the case, the sense of purpose that human beings have in their intentions and voluntary actions is an illusion and any belief in a more long-term purpose in evolution is entirely mistaken.

3. On the contrary, the course of human history in this case is no more than a continuation of the competition for survival manifest in evolution, and hence competition for resources, involving inequality, violence and war, is a necessary corollary of this process and cannot be avoided.

4. Religions, supposedly the reflection of human appreciation of a higher reality beyond the physical, in reality originate from the desire for control and success, and themselves foster the competition, inequality, violence and war that such a desire generates. They invoke, on slender evidence, special knowledge of a supernatural being or beings outside the physical world in which we live and of a life beyond the physical existence we experience, and by competing claims to know the truth about winning through to such a life, they generate further disputes and violence. Their offer is not to the whole world but to the individual, how to find your happiness, your freedom, your fulfilment. Do this and you will experience life in a way you have never lived before, they all claim.

5. Many who believe in the urgent need for a better deal for the suffering and underprivileged as a practical or political philosophy remain sceptical that creation is anything other than an inevitable sequence of cause and effect without purpose from its beginning and on through the struggles of evolution and competition for survival between individuals and human societies. For them, the wish for a better deal is driven by compassion arising from the suffering they see around them, rather than any sense of a design in creation and an ultimate purpose for humanity, to which their choices and actions can contribute. The question is then, "Why bother?" If all feelings of freedom and ability to choose and to change things are in reality illusory and life has no ultimate purpose then it is tempting to conclude that nothing "matters" really, and attempting to alleviate

the lot of those who get a raw deal is simply swimming against an inevitable tide.

And yet there is still a yearning for something more, a belief in purpose and the possibility of progress not merely devoted to control of the physical world. Often, as we have seen, this is only individualistic, but not always and not entirely. Where does this originate? Is it a mere illusion? Do things have to stay like this and, if so, will humanity live to tell the tale? We propose here to invite perusal of some of the ideas of a person who thought life could be worth living, especially if human beings would take the trouble to understand their own nature and its enormous potential for future development, and to change their priorities. It is not surprising that people found him at times bewildering, at times downright threatening, at others just incomprehensible. Intelligence and learning did not then and do not now, guarantee understanding and wisdom. Knowing how the physical world works and even how human brains work, does not tell us how we can best live in the world. This requires wisdom of a very different sort, and in this book we will be investigating a source of such wisdom, Jesus of Nazareth.

Jesus presented a very different picture of the nature, purpose and potential of human life from those we have been considering. "Ah," you may think, "so we are back to religion, despite the condemnation of its influence above! Surely Christianity has all the qualities rejected earlier and is responsible for as many misdeeds as any other religion." With this we do not disagree, but the case we wish to present is that we have to disentangle Jesus from the religion which was created by human beings who used him as a starting point for one more variation on the religious theme, with magic formulae for salvation, an institution to organise the special group, special rules for adherents and hostility to the outsider. The teaching of Jesus, we claim, has none of this, nor does it see God as anything like the gods of other religions, an authority figure to be feared and placated. It does indeed assume a God and all Jesus' teaching emanates from his understanding of the nature of that God, and a purpose for humanity, but both God and purpose differ radically from the conventions of human religions. The church has so often seen the primary purpose as one of getting its members to heaven by ensuring that they follow the rules, despite simultaneously preaching a strange doctrine of atonement to which we will come in due course, which asserts that only believing and not observation of prescribed rituals is required. We will argue that Jesus' teaching makes sense (in fact more sense) in the context we now know of evolution and human existence. He talks about what we might call a further "evolution" of humanity to a higher state and a better life, both in the physical world here and a non-physical mode of existence which is outside our understanding. He also, far from suggesting that everything has been done for our salvation and only our assent is required (the traditional Christian theme), implies that humans must "come of age" (in a phrase of the German theologian, Dietrich Bonhoeffer), and take responsibility for their own future as developed adults.

All this, of course, presupposes much that, as we have already admitted, has apparently been discounted by science – a creator, freedom and purpose, a reality outside our physical world. These issues we will address in due course, but first we propose to look carefully at Jesus, his teaching and his example, to justify our case that he should be detached from the religious framework into which he has been so deeply embedded.

Jesus' proposed alternative to competition and individualism as the way of running the world has never been seriously tested. It is that we each put the needs of all others, not just our immediate circle, on a par with, or even above, the needs of ourselves. This alone, he teaches, reflects what God is like and can provide the route to a better existence, in which humanity can change radically in ways that we will elaborate as our argument proceeds. It offers a solution to the manifold threats to humanity's future. The search for and practice of this love for others requires giving up the search each for our own satisfaction, yet paradoxically it alone provides a means to the true satisfaction of the longings we all have, even those who are least aware of them. This principle of love for all implies huge changes in the human approach to politics, commerce, science, technology, work, the environment and many other aspects of life. We will be examining the need to change in more detail as we continue. The principle refuses to see individuals in isolation, each seeking his or her own salvation by some specific formula or ritual. Rather it seeks a universal raising of humanity to a better way of living.

We emphatically do not wish to present this alternative approach as one more attempt to construct a better religion. Though having the experience of a Christian background, we do not see our aim as an attempt to reform Christianity (in any of its myriad forms), because, like all religions, institutional Christianity embodies fatal flaws which preclude the attainment of this higher fulfilment for humanity. As well as the divisiveness to which we have already referred, religions encourage and depend on longings for certainty and security and offer assurances that all things can be well in another state after death, even if they are far from perfect in this world; hence they tend to emphasise the "spiritual" as against the "physical" aspects of life. But, we will argue, human growth requires uncertainty and change, which are so obviously present throughout evolution and have not suddenly ceased to operate. And, if we accept that there may be some purpose at work in the universe, this physical life is surely not just a meaningless interlude before some state of heavenly bliss, but has its own function and point. While we agree with the religious emphasis that life has more than a physical dimension, there is a risk that this will lead to a neglect of the physical dimension, in a narrow fixation with "the other world". Jesus spent most of his time talking about life in the physical world and we need to consider his teaching as relating to the world we know and in which we live. Evolution has been a continuous process of change in the physical world and has produced humanity. Any understanding of a purpose for life must, we suggest, take account of the evolutionary process and interpret the future in terms that make sense in the light of that process. The physical and the spiritual are not two separate modes of existence that can be stressed in isolation from each other by science on the one hand or by religion on the other, but they are indissolubly related.

Jesus asserted that God is essentially a God of love with a deep concern for all mankind. To the reader who may want to say, "Rubbish! If God were a God of love, this would never have happened to ...", we would say, "Imagine what the world would be like if everything that one person did not want was prevented from happening. Such a world would be impossible for ordinary human mortals, for the claims of one to a veto would have to allow the claims of all others."

While we may no longer feel able to blame the Devil for all the ills we see, we have other excuses to offer, such as the power of the genes or "the market" or the pressures of life. While we will be attempting to expose the weakness of these excuses, we would not, of course, wish to deny that disadvantages of environment and upbringing (compounded by low levels of mutual support in a society organised competitively rather than co-operatively) seriously damage the capacity of some individuals to achieve their potential for adulthood. We are all, to some degree, impaired by the world as it is, yet we will argue that all nevertheless retain at least some capacity for choice and jointly we need to recognise this and consider the alternatives set before humanity as a whole. In this book we are arguing that, far from our additional knowledge offering us more excuses for our incompetence, this knowledge has brought us to a point where many of us can be more fully aware of the consequences of our actions and can better understand the wisdom about the human condition offered 2000 years ago by Jesus. We need to take up his challenge to accept responsibility as adults for each other and our world as a whole. We can put aside earlier misinterpretation of what he said and use his help to take a huge practical step toward a better state of things. We are, therefore, attempting to see Jesus' message against the background of modern knowledge about the universe and our world as a practical programme for the improvement of human happiness.

Chapter 2
The World We Live In

Recent history

The 20th century saw the greatest advances ever in ability to manipulate the physical environment to the advantage of humanity, but the benefits were restricted, and large areas of the globe, involving huge numbers of people, saw very little of the benefits, except for small elites holding power, often by dubious means. Even in the prosperous areas of the globe, prosperity did not bring peace. The advance to greater comfort in life was punctuated by horrendous episodes of destructive conflict affecting vast populations. In the First World War 21 million died and in the Second World War 55 million (20 million in Russia alone). Subsequently, in the last half of the century, the major ideological conflict between capitalism and state communism was fought out by substitutes and clients in the poorer areas of the world, such as Asia, South America and Africa.

While, even in the rich countries, poverty was not eliminated, the numbers suffering extreme poverty in those countries were nevertheless reduced, and some form of state support was provided, albeit often inadequately, to prevent destitution. However, in effect, poverty was often exported to countries where desperation meant that human beings would accept scandalous conditions and wages to produce the goods which even the less well-off in the richer countries could now afford, often at prices which concealed a huge mark-up to the benefit, not of the poor producers, but the transport and sales sectors based in the richer world which provided the capital, then transported and sold the products of poverty. The exploitation of the poor and weak thus continued on a much greater scale than had applied in the 19th century when the industrial revolution in Britain first enabled large-scale production of a large range of goods.

The terrorist attacks in New York have made the promises of a peaceful and prosperous "new order" (so facilely promulgated after the collapse of the Berlin Wall and the disappearance of the Russian empire in Eastern Europe) look as unreal as impartial observers always suspected them to be. In reality these promises marked western (primarily American) determination to promote their business and political power across the globe rather than true justice, democracy and equality. Andrew Natsios, the Administrator of the United States International Aid Agency, the body responsible for co-ordinating American financial "assistance" to the poor countries of the world, states on the Agency's website that, "America's foreign assistance both serves to accomplish our foreign policy objectives, and expresses the deep humanitarian instincts of the American people". Note the order of priorities. It might also be noted that as a percentage of the national income America's aid programme is the meanest of any "developed" country. The consequences of this economic imperialism are now beginning to emerge.

The end of the Soviet Union, far from liberating its peoples, led to total collapse of the economy and beggary for most people. Under the insistence of America that a market economy must be introduced, with little financial support from the west to implement such a massive change, unemployment mushroomed, extreme inequalities developed, organised crime took over large sectors of the economy and public assets were sold off in a flood of corruption. National income fell by over 50% and the number of citizens living below the poverty line rose from 14 million in 1989 to 147 million in 1998, in which year a further financial crash followed. Almost at a stroke, many developing countries found that they had no champion to support them in resisting capitalist economic imperialism and the spread of multinational domination. Not many years later the Japanese economic miracle began to falter and has never recovered, demonstrating that the system is far from perfect.

Salvation by the market

Despite these failures, the theory in which we are still urged to put our faith is that "the market" provides the simplest and most effective mechanism for ensuring that the needs of all humanity are met. Demand for some product, claims the theory, whether it be as basic as grain or as complex as a vaccine for Aids, will inevitably ensure that someone invests resources in meeting this need in order to earn a profit from the labour involved in developing, producing and marketing the product. There is, however, a fatal flaw in this theory. It assumes that producing the required product will be more attractive (which usually means more profitable) than producing something else. Frequently this situation does not exist, for the following reason. However great the need for a product, such as a medicine for malaria, unless resources are available to exchange for it, there is no incentive to produce it. Simple need is not enough. The necessary resources can only be available through work or existing capital. The poor, by definition, have no capital. They do, of course, have their labour to offer, but if it is not in demand they have nothing with which to bargain. And increasingly labour is a poor bargaining counter, because capital can use technology to ensure that few hands produce enough to meet the current demand and can play off the poor in one part of the world against those in another when hiring labour. Hence capital holds nearly all the cards and increasingly funnels the earth's resources into its own pockets. Money, a tool originally devised to aid the interchange of goods to the benefit of all, has been perverted into a tyrannical system used by the few to control the many. The world financial system has become the most pervasive example of the dominance of selfish competition in the life of the modern world. The market can never meet the needs of the most needy, though it works very effectively for those with good initial resources. (For a detailed discussion of the philosophy and failings of the market, see Jenkins, 2000).

In the last decade the application of this theory of the market has spread like wildfire across the globe (globalisation) and the world economy has become still more dominated by financial systems under the control of the rich countries and a relatively small number of multinational companies based in the rich world but operating across many different countries with a co-ordinated policy. We are continually told by our leaders in "the west" that international trade will contribute to the prosperity of all, whether they are initially rich or poor, and that all obstacles to the freedom of such trade must be removed. But the removal of these "obstacles" has usually meant that restrictions on the operation of global companies are removed, enabling them to penetrate weaker economies and destroy local producers and traders. (Even within Britain we can see the same trend as supermarket chains take advantage of the relaxation of restrictions to take over an increasing range of provision, putting small local shops out of business and driving down the returns to the producers.) Local agriculture in weaker economies loses out to exports of agricultural surpluses from the rich countries, often subsidised by the taxpayer, protecting their own agriculture from competition while insisting that such protection is removed by their poor competitors. The theory that wealth created (it is claimed) by the better-off will in due course "trickle down" to the poor has been shown to be a cynical misrepresentation of what really happens. On the contrary, profits are funnelled from the poor to the rich world. Reciprocal removal of barriers operating to prevent access by the poor producers to the markets of the rich are either refused or promised but remain unimplemented. While it is proclaimed that the aim of this globalisation process is to enable competition on a level playing field, so that inefficiency will be driven out by better methods, in practice no level playing field is provided, and even if it were, the initial power of the competitors is loaded inexorably in favour of those already better off, irrespective of how efficient or otherwise they may be. But even if all producers were equal competitors at the start, not all have equal power to buy. The theory that "the market" will ensure that needs are met in the most efficient manner is deeply flawed because producers will only produce for those who can afford to buy, not for those whose need is greatest. Hence luxury products like Coke and trainers and slimming aids have huge resources devoted to them, while fundamental needs like clean water and medicines to deal with widespread diseases of the poor do not. We have a global economy, but not an economy for the whole globe. Rather it divides the globe into haves and have-nots. Furthermore, market forces are only allowed to operate freely when their operation tallies with the interests of the powerful. Poor countries have not been allowed to default on their debts to the rich countries, but when the financial crisis in Japan and Korea in 1997 threatened the investments of the rich, large injections of funds were rapidly mobilised to save the system from its own mistakes.

Proponents of capitalism will argue that it creates the wealth from which taxation is enabled to draw resources to be used for the support of the poor. But the creation of such profits may well have contributed to the poverty in question. Company taxation (which in any case many multinational companies reduce to a minimum by switching funds around the world) is only possible because profits are large enough to bear it, while also keeping shareholders happy. Ability to meet taxation depends, ultimately, on charging customers as much as possible and paying workers as little as possible, so it can hardly be claimed as an inherent virtue of the system. Rather taxation is a means of restoring to some extent the imbalances which the process embodies, and which a different economic system could reduce by operating in a manner fairer to all.

So even the basic needs of the poor and dispossessed exert no influence because they do not have the wherewithal to trade in return for what they need. Their labour in practice means very little in a world where technology available to the rich means that too many hands pursue too few jobs across the whole globe and the many hands have no assets such as land which they can exploit. Instead of the development of technology ensuring that all would benefit from a reduced burden of physical work, in practice we find fewer people working, and working long hours, and many without access to any work at all. Technology delivers more power to the already powerful and so is introduced even when it is not of general benefit and will destroy the livelihoods of many. Hence the needs of the poor can only be met with the co-operation or consent and active support of the rich and powerful. In the short term this looks like a demand for pure altruism and receives fairly short shrift. Altruism is in short supply, especially among those who wield the power, and in any case allowing altruism to dictate policies would deny the supposed beneficence of the market. Yet in the long run neglecting these needs may reap its own unpleasant reward.

A further consequence of this philosophy is the widespread damage to the global environment on which all of us, rich and poor, depend and on which our children and grandchildren will in turn depend. The poor damage their environment in a desperate search for such essential materials as firewood and the rich damage it in a search for yet more resources to meet galloping demand for an even higher standard of living. Long-term consequences of destroying forests and burning fossil fuels are disregarded in the interests of immediate profit and immediate short-term benefits for the consumer in the form of cheap goods. Originally ignorance of the consequences of this way of life was a legitimate excuse, but that time has long passed and the causes and effects of pollution, desertification and climate change are now well established and the threats to the quality of human life, even for the rich, are understood. Yet many oil companies still deny the link between the burning of fossil fuels and global warming, together with the likely long-term effects of such warming. And the will to do anything about this progress to degradation is notably lacking and the interests of those who "trade" remain paramount in international conferences. Powerful interests in the oil industry have worked hard to delay development of technology to exploit renewable energy resources. In 2000 President Bush refused to sign the Kyoto agreement on reduction of carbon emissions on the grounds that national commercial considerations were more important, that is the enrichment of (some) Americans outweighed the future effects of climate destabilisation on the whole of humanity. And the USA, with only about 4% of the world's population, produces 25% of the world's pollution. Even where restrictions have been attempted, they are widely flouted, for example by illegal logging and mining practices.

Certainly in the last 50 years we have achieved the capability of satisfying legitimate desires for all, not merely in "the north" but across the whole globe. But this capability has not been matched by a will to share these benefits equally, and in those who have benefited the "legitimate" desires have not remained static. Expectations have risen and desire for individual advancement and success has grown rather than receded as the initial needs became more easily satisfied. While overt international violence has only infrequently been necessary to maintain the advantages of the rich and powerful, more subtle and effective methods have been deployed in the guise of international "agreements" to ensure that prosperity continued to grow in the rich world, while the basic needs of many elsewhere remained unmet or their condition even grew worse.

The market at work

Hardly a day passes without some example emerging of the amoral pursuit of short-term profit and its consequences or the distortion or concealment of truth in support of such pursuit. We present a few of the more striking recent examples.

In 1984 a pesticides factory run by Union Carbide, a United States multinational, exploded at Bhopal in India. The streets were filled with bodies and half a million people were injured by the poisonous gases released by the explosion. Over twenty years later virtually nothing has been done by Union Carbide (or Dow Chemical which bought the company later) for the victims, though the company had assets of billions. The company offer amounted to less than $800 per person (less than half the average annual wage). Over 100,000 people are still critically ill, unable to work and dreadful effects on babies still continue. The site has never been cleaned up and continues to poison the groundwater.

Until quite recently those who had worked in the asbestos industry and developed mesothelioma, the fatal lung disease resulting from inhalation of asbestos fibres, could assume that liability would be shared between their past employers, very many of whom had been negligent and ignored safety regulations introduced once the threat of asbestos was known. However this is no longer so, since in 2001 the Appeal Court upheld an earlier judgement that any case against previous employers must prove that the "fatal fibre" (i.e. the one which initiated the disease) was inhaled while working for that particular employer rather than any other. Since most of those affected had worked for more than one employer, this was impossible, so none of the employers could be forced to take responsibility. Hence many dying men have failed to achieve any compensation to support their dependents.

In 2000 a consortium of the biggest and wealthiest drug companies in the world sought to prevent South Africa from producing or importing cheaper versions of patent medicines to combat Aids, which is pandemic in the country. They were not at the time prepared to licence such production, though their own versions were far too costly for the country to afford. Meanwhile people died in their thousands and the epidemic spread more widely. Profits, not need, ruled, though some specious arguments were presented that in the long run the companies had the interests of the sufferers at heart. Public opinion across the globe was so outraged that the companies eventually realised they were on a loser, and backed down. The sequel, however, has been that quantities of drugs supplied at a reduced price to Africa have been siphoned off illegally and resold in Europe at huge profits (*The Guardian*, 31 October 2002).

Also in 2000 (*The Guardian*, 17 July 2001) Philip Morris, leading producers of cigarettes, now seeking new markets in Eastern Europe and Asia because demand had fallen in countries where the fatal consequences of their product were better known, suggested to the Czech government that encouraging cigarette sales would benefit the economy because deaths of smokers at a younger age would reduce the need to pay state pensions. For years the tobacco companies also denied the link between smoking and cancer (and other diseases). They now recognise it (see, for example, the British American Tobacco Social Report 2001/1) but argue that there is nothing wrong with continuing to manufacture and sell cigarettes.

And, in a more general example of the focus of modern medicine, Médecins sans Frontières wrote to 20 major drug companies to discover what medicines they were developing for the prevailing diseases among the world's poor. None of the 11 companies who replied had produced a drug in the previous five years for malaria, tuberculosis, sleeping sickness or several other less well-known but equally deadly threats. Less than 1% of budget was being spent on such diseases. In contrast eight new drugs were on offer for impotence and seven for obesity, the "scourges" of the rich world.

Thirteen out of 1233 drugs patented from 1975–1997 were for tropical diseases (George and Wilding, 2002). In 1999 a drug which effectively treated sleeping sickness, eflomithine, was withdrawn from production because the victims could not afford it. Production was later resumed when it was found to be useful in hair-removing creams. Yet, to quote Harvard economist Jeffrey Sachs, "Millions and millions of people are dying every year in poor countries of conditions that are absolutely preventable and treatable if we pay some attention" (*The Guardian*, 21 December 2001).

A striking example of official concealment of the truth for commercial purposes is the Spanish epidemic of so-called "toxic oil syndrome". Beginning in 1981, over 1000 people died and over 25,000 were seriously affected by a mysterious illness which was officially attributed to rapeseed oil contaminated with aniline. This oil was allowed into Spain only for industrial use in order to protect the olive oil industry and was made inedible through the aniline additive. It was, however, widely sold illegally on the streets for human consumption, being much cheaper than olive oil. Hence it offered a ready-made explanation for the epidemic. However Bob Woffinden (*The Guardian*, 25 August 2001) described a lengthy investigation and concluded that an official government cover-up of the real cause of the epidemic had been mounted to protect Spanish agriculture. Less than two weeks after the first case, the head of endocrinology at La Paz hospital published a newspaper article pointing out that the symptoms were similar to those due to organo-phosphate poisoning. He was ordered by the health ministry to say no more. The same day, Dr Antonio Muro, whose staff at Madrid's clinic for infectious diseases had treated some early cases, after examining the distribution of cases and their common features, tried to convince health ministry officials that contaminated food rather than oil was responsible, but for his pains he was dismissed from his post as hospital director. Subsequently he tested samples of oil from affected families and found they all differed so could not be the source of a single pattern of symptoms. Enrique Genique, the secretary of state for consumer affairs, found there was no relation between areas where the oil was sold and where the disease occurred, but he was also sacked when he presented these results to the health ministry. Two other scientists, who initially believed the oil theory, were appointed in 1983 to write another report, and came to a similar conclusion to Genique but were also sacked. Meanwhile, Antonio Muro was pursuing his own enquiries and had concluded that tomatoes contaminated with organo-phosphate pesticides were the real cause. They came from Almeria, a former desert area transformed for crops by the discovery of underground water, where rapid growth of the crops was dependent on copious use of chemicals. To acknowledge that this supposed agricultural miracle was the source of the disease would have had disastrous implications for agricultural exports and tourism. Yet an internal German government memo was leaked to the magazine *Der Spiegel* 20 years later, which revealed that unsafe pesticide residues were still being found in fruit and vegetables imported from Spain. But, said the memo, "Under no circumstances should the general public be informed".

Three areas where the pursuit of commercial interests at the expense of human need have been most glaringly apparent have been international debt, arms sales and environmental degradation.

The international debt crisis originates from the 1960s, when oil producers hugely increased oil prices and recycled the resulting financial surplus to western banks. To employ these surpluses the banks (and governments) made generous loans to poorer countries without too systematic an investigation of the use to which the money would be put or what would serve as collateral in case of failure to repay. Interest rates rose in the next decade, the recipient countries found themselves faced with increased payments to service the debts, which had rarely been used for sound development projects and had all too often been frittered away on unproductive schemes such as arms purchases or technology, which could not be maintained in working order, or they had disappeared into private accounts of members of the ruling class. Furthermore, the trading policies of the rich were simultaneously designed to hinder any efforts of the poor to earn the wherewithal to pay off the debt, by cutting the price paid for the goods the poor could sell abroad (primarily unprocessed and hence perishable agricultural products in competition with other countries in a similarly weak position) and raising the prices of the manufactured goods which the poor were desperate to buy to help create the infrastructure for development. Tariff walls around rich countries also hindered the ability of the poor to develop a manufacturing sector in order to export processed goods instead of the raw materials to which they were largely restricted.

As the crisis deepened, the international community in the shape of the International Monetary Fund and the World Bank, both dominated by the developed world, enforced Structural Adjustment Policies to stabilise the economies of the debt-ridden poor world. These policies were designed to ensure that the debts could continue to be serviced, whatever the cost to the poorer citizens of the indebted countries, by requiring strict restraints on public spending. Poor countries were forced to cut or completely withdraw free education and health, subsidies on basic foodstuffs were removed and agriculture directed to grow export crops rather than food for local consumption. Thus the poor of the developing world were penalised for the improvident lending of western banks and governments and the self-serving inefficiency of their own rulers. What is more, the policies largely failed even to achieve the goals of those who imposed them. Poor countries were forced to grow cash crops in competition with each other, producing world surpluses and forcing down prices. Though the original debts have been paid off many times in interest, the creditors continue to demand payment on loans that will never in reality be repaid.

The biggest international arms exporters have consistently been the USA, Britain, France and Germany. The arms trade, originally fuelled by the Cold War and the paranoiac insistence of the USA on supporting any government with declared anti-communist leanings, however dubious its human rights credentials, has been reduced somewhat but by no means eliminated with the end of the Cold War. There remains a flourishing trade in arms of every type, sold officially to governments for self-defence, even where no enemy is apparent on the horizon, but often used to subdue unrest among the state's own citizens, or finding their way illegally to rebel movements of various kinds which have been thrown up by the instability stemming from inequality and injustice. According to a recent report by Amnesty International, supporters of Osama Bin-Laden have been able to buy American-made arms in Pakistan as recently as 2001. The G8 group of countries (the biggest world economies) sell £19 billion-worth of arms a year to "developing" nations, according to the same report. They then castigate the latter for poor economic management! Britain has shipped arms to apartheid South Africa, Pinochet's government in Chile, Iran and Iraq and continues to sell to China, Indonesia, Turkey and Saudi Arabia, all countries with highly dubious human rights records. During the period of extreme tension between India and Pakistan over Kashmir in 2002, Tony Blair went on a "peace mission" to the subcontinent, the main focus of which appeared to be a 1 billion sale of fighter bombers to India. The combined annual military expenditure of the two countries is about $8 billion, while 40% of their people live in poverty.

In Britain, arms exports have received for mysterious reasons special government support in the form of the Defence (sic) Sales Organisation, which guarantees exporters against defaults on payment (not infrequent in the unstable areas of the world where many arms sales occur) with taxpayers' money. The argument has been that arms manufacturers have only a limited market in sales to their own government, so they need other outlets to maintain their viability, and also that if we were not selling the arms to some dubious dictator, other governments would be doing it. The permanent subsidy that this entails is quietly disregarded. Economists commonly argue that the reasons for the policy must be political and security concerns because the economics make no sense, while politicians commonly argue from irrational economic grounds such as those above. Ironically in several conflicts around the world (notably in the Falklands, Iraq and Sierra Leone), British troops have found themselves confronted with weapons made in Britain and sold legitimately or illegitimately to their current enemies. This short-sighted and financially absurd policy has contributed to a considerable degree to the continual instability of the trouble spots of the world, providing the fuel to keep conflicts burning, whereas devoting the same funds to more productive ends in the same areas might well have reduced or even solved these conflicts.

The pursuit of commercial gain has fostered environmental destruction right across the globe. Mining companies and oil companies have extracted wealth in many "developing" countries, almost none of which finds its way to the local people, leaving toxic waste and poisoned rivers. Demand for timber in the rich world has encouraged logging, often illegal, which removes irreplaceable and rare species of trees, causing erosion, breakdown of soil structure, loss of habitats and species and destruction of resources previously used sustainably by the local people. In the Niger delta activities of oil companies have enriched the Nigerian government, while often destroying the environment on which the local people depend.

The claim that these trends threaten the very future of humanity is not just a wild idea of eccentric doom-mongers. The 2003 State of the World Report from the Washington-based Worldwatch Institute states that we have one or maybe two generations to rescue ourselves. The report points to the crises in food production in many countries, land degradation, global warming, release of toxic chemicals, movements of invasive species to areas where they have no natural predators and the loss of life-support systems and living species.

Life of the individual

So much, then, for the effects of public exercise of the free market, with its competition for resources and customers. No-one can deny that this process has enriched many millions in prosperous countries of the world (often now referred to as "the north"), providing the cars and household appliances on which we all now depend. We live in comfort, very many of us, but these benefits are not equally spread even within our own countries and communities. Nor is there much sign that, once a certain standard of living has been reached, the average person will sigh with satisfaction and say "enough is enough – it's time to help the less well-off ". On the contrary, there is always someone else with something more as a model for further aspiration and once a sufficiently large number of the electorate achieves a certain level of prosperity under the competitive system, they will cease to support any change toward a system in which the better-off take more responsibility for the poor through generous benefits and support funded by taxation. People work longer and longer hours in order to own more and more and barely have time to enjoy it. There has been a huge increase in the number of working days lost to stress, which now amount to far more than the losses due to strikes. Those with the power in commerce award themselves bigger and bigger salaries and bonuses (one wonders what they can do with such huge amounts, especially given the hours they claim to work) and always the producers seek for some new twist, some extra titillation to add to their product which will give it the edge over a rival or encourage customers to throw out the old and switch to the new. More and more of the world's resources end up on rubbish tips, rather than being used profitably, because the system requires consumers to keep spending and uses every trick it knows to encourage them to do so. And because they are persuaded they need to spend on themselves, they resist withdrawal of their money in the form of taxes to be spent for the general good.

More and more families own one car or two or three, yet motorists persistently lament the stress of travel. Supermarkets, by exercising tight control over prices paid to producers, can maintain low prices and encourage people to drive long distances for the weekly shopping. They also ship products, usually by air, from all over the globe, increasing environmental pollution and, with their economic strength, play vulnerable producers off against each other. News items regularly announce that a company is opening a new store, creating so many hundred jobs, as if demand were infinitely elastic and no jobs will be lost through the competition. Yet local shops, especially in villages, are persistently driven out of business, leaving the elderly and disabled with formidable problems of access to resources. Those with cars drive to work because it is the quickest mode of travel, and drive to the gym in order to counter the effects of an inactive lifestyle. Obesity has become a major health problem. Drivers argue for more roads, but the new roads are soon as choked with traffic as the old ones. Cars pollute the air by their use and gobble resources for their creation, leaving poisons behind in the process, and then leave problems of disposing of them when they are replaced by newer models.

Instead of local schools catering for local children, a struggle for survival has also been introduced into the educational environment in Britain. Schools compete frenetically for the academically most promising pupils and schools with a good reputation can draw pupils from long distances, usually driven to school by car and further choking the roads. Even though non-selective education produces better all-round results, selection is being re-introduced covertly under the guise of "specialist" schools and "city academies", which are given extra funding and ultimately deprive the rest of funds where they are needed most to cater for the children who lose out due to poor home and social environment (see Polly Toynbee, *The Guardian*, 6 December 2002). At the local level, education authorities are pressured by more vocal groups to spend money on improving local schools for example, certainly not a bad aim. But often this means that a more vulnerable group with less political clout, such as those needing the help of Social Services, will find that provision for their needs is cut. More competitive still, the better-off will frequently seek to buy private and supposedly better education and health care. They are then unwilling to pay adequate taxation to support national educational, health and transport services and the level of taxation becomes a major election issue with parties vying to promise the lowest taxes, rather than the best services. The priority of concern for self first and foremost will of course inexorably be passed on to children from an early age. Many young children see little of their fathers (where there is one present in the family) due to long working hours and long journeys to work, often due to living in a "nice" area while working far away in a city centre. Possessions and money and big presents at Christmas are stressed as the key to life, rather than love and play and doing things together.

Education is increasingly seen solely as the means to a good job, rather than an opportunity to develop all aspects of the child (and adult). Schools are labelled good or bad depending on narrow test results and become desirable or otherwise in consequence. Their main role, in the eyes of governments, now seems to be to train for success in a competitive society, not to inculcate a sharing and supportive interdependence or to provoke critical thought about the society, its good and bad features and how it might change for the better. There is little debate about the purpose of education, whether it should impart life skills and values, stimulate children to be able to live a full and purposeful life, teach them how to appreciate art and culture, or even its role in helping children to cope with the more mundane aspects of life like how to avoid pregnancy, read a train timetable and plan their finances. There has been almost no investigation or consideration of whether inculcating a totally different ethos from that which dominates at present might eventually lead to a happier society.

The pursuit of riches seems to have become the sole purpose of life. The chief executive of the huge drugs group GlaxoSmithKline was reported recently as feeling underpaid at £7 million per annum and was asking for a massive increase to keep him motivated (*The Guardian*, 18 November 2002). Though humans have always competed for power and riches, only comparatively recently has this become such a dominant goal of the majority of the population (many of whom cite "shopping" as their main hobby). In the USA and, increasingly, in Britain, though less so in the rest of Europe, the stock market dominates the business sector. The sole role of a business is seen as providing higher and higher returns on shares. The proportion of profits paid out in dividends has doubled since 1960 in the USA, reducing investment for growth, research and development (Hutton, 2002), not to mention better wages. Thus the interests of those who already have wealth dominate, and the interests of other stakeholders (workers and customers and others affected by a company's activities) have less and less influence.

Selfish competition in the guise of promoting efficiency will seek to keep prices low and the wages of workers low in consequence, with poor or non-existent pension provision. The main focus is on the price of a product and the profit that can be made on it, to keep the shareholders happy, not whether it has been produced by workers who are given a fair deal. Workers are frequently brought in to the richer countries from the "developing" world to do the jobs in agriculture, hospitals and catering which are paid so badly that no native workers will take them. Yet refugees from even worse conditions abroad which the system exacerbates (and even those fleeing violent persecution) are regarded as spongers and a threat. The dominance of the selfish, competitive, acquisitive system based on money infects all life like a virus. Like Midas, we will surely find that our competitive pursuit of wealth finally turns sour on us.

In Britain inequality has increased markedly across the whole income range in the last two decades and this country is now the most unequal society in Europe in terms of earnings and has the worst public services, despite being the fourth (or fifth) largest economy in the world. The USA, the richest country in the world, is even more unequal with even worse public services (1% of the population owns 38% of the wealth). And inequality within a country is associated with the level of discontent in the population. Individualism has exacerbated our difficulty in living with each other and the demand for separate dwellings for smaller family units exacerbates the apparently permanent problem in Britain of providing decent housing for all. At the other end of the housing market, prices are driven up by the huge increases in salaries gained by executives in recent years, but increasingly the rich have to fortify their houses with burglar detection and controlled entry systems against the threat of burglary or worse. These needs are even more glaring in wealthy areas of America or South Africa, where the contrasts between rich and poor are greater, and dwellings end up resembling armed forts. America stubbornly resists any control of gun ownership, while 25,000 Americans a year die from guns. Meanwhile the prison population has more than tripled since 1980.

In Britain too, the most prevalent attitude to crime is retaliatory, rather than constructive and effective. Our judicial system is focussed on the notion of retaliation, whatever the ideals may be said to be. The need to give space and opportunity to develop a more productive and rewarding life as an alternative to crime is unpopular and therefore under-resourced and is regarded as a soft option even though in the long run it may offer much greater security for the community. Prisons are vastly overcrowded and therefore merely compound the problems that they are supposed to combat and provide little deterrent. Despite this, there is a constant auction between political parties to prove that each is tougher on crime than the other, bowing to public demand for a simple self-righteous answer to the perceived threat. In California a third offence as trivial as stealing a pizza will incur a 25-year prison sentence. Apparently society does not jib at paying the costs of prison, yet is reluctant to direct resources into more creative ways of coping. Victims of crimes persistently complain that the guilty have been let off lightly. Prison can be imposed for a single act of negligence without deliberate malice, as in recent cases involving a surgeon who gave the wrong instruction to a subordinate which resulted in the patient's death and a teacher leading an adventure course, who gave an order to a boy which led to his drowning. Foolish and irresponsible as these actions can be seen to be in retrospect, they were not the result of evil intention and left their perpetrators scarred for the rest of their lives. Retribution (for this is all that imprisonment can be in such a case) offers no opportunity to recompense society, in however small a way, for the damage caused. It merely forces society to pay to keep a man in prison in pursuit of a meaningless act of revenge. The same is true of another recent case where a paedophile was sent to prison for acts he had committed 25 years earlier, even though he had since struggled to overcome his inappropriate behaviour and was living a useful and reformed life. The judge commended him for this but still committed him to prison, with the risk of undoing all that the man had achieved. Where was the sense in that? This is not to say that prison, with proper support and retraining and treatment, may not be the right answer in some cases to protect society or reform the guilty. But more resources need to be directed to identifying and remedying the underlying causes of so much crime. That requires a huge change of attitudes.

And then there is the drugs problem. Sixty per cent of those in prison are there for drug-related offences and a huge proportion of police time is occupied in dealing with drug offenders (even more if alcohol-related crime is included). Drugs are a way of escape from the boredom or the problems of life, or they are a way to achieve some form of enlightenment or ecstasy or escape to a "high". Their popularity demonstrates the inability of our society to provide a satisfying and fulfilling life to so many and the simultaneous pursuit of individual and instant gratification. Such gratification is, of course, only temporary and leads to hell on earth, if access to the drug is then prevented, and crime to obtain the wherewithal to feed the habit. The drugs trade is also fostered by the unjust world economic system. As farmers in many a poor country have found, world trade policies can destroy an honest living from growing food crops, but it is highly profitable to grow opium or coca, which can be exported to Europe or America to feed the demand and increase the problems of the developed world in turn. The greater the success in intercepting the import of drugs into our country, the higher the prices on the street and the more crime is required of addicts to feed their habit. Hence we are hoist with our own petard.

In summary, though in the last 100 years the physical comforts of life have improved for many, differences in wealth and income have increased hugely and numbers in absolute poverty have not decreased. The basic reason for this situation is that, at least in "western" society, the driving force is the desire to acquire not merely enough for a reasonably comfortable life, but ever more of the goods which human ingenuity creates. This continues even though more goods do not produce more happiness and even though it thereby denies a reasonable sufficiency to many others. In two words, greed and selfishness appear to be the mainsprings of much current human activity. This situation ultimately affects not only the deprived but also the deprivers, for it creates directly or indirectly the problems of violence, insecurity and environmental degradation which we have been considering. In the next chapter we look at suggestions for a different way of doing things.

Chapter 3
A Different Approach

Jesus of Nazareth urged and lived a very different way of life from that we have been considering. He claimed to represent God and to offer God's way for all human beings to live a full and fulfilling life. "Change your priorities, raise your sights, look at life in a different way," he constantly urged. The focus of the change is to be the realisation that it is not the self but "the other" that is of fundamental importance to fulfilment. Life was designed by God for something more than merely acquiring possessions and status. We will explore these themes in more detail and their implication for the practicalities of economics, politics, social relations and so on. As already indicated, Jesus presents them as reflecting the nature and purpose of a creator God. This basis of his teaching we will examine later, but for the present we focus on his teachings as practical proposals for everyday human intercourse rather than a template for religion (necessarily in presenting Jesus' words directly at times, reference to God cannot be excluded).

Change in priorities

A prevailing theme of Jesus' teaching is the need for human nature to change. Though he does not, of course, express the theme in terms of evolution, we can easily interpret it in those terms. The assumptions and motives that have evolved in human thinking during the long process of evolution and have served in reaching the current state must be abandoned and replaced if further progress is to occur. The step to a "higher plane" of existence, it seems, will not occur by the well-tried route of chance and competition to survive, because that route has left us with a legacy of accelerating conflicts and threats of disaster (economic, political, social and ecological). The new advance can perhaps come at this point in history because human understanding has reached a point where it can affect its own destiny more directly. However, this necessarily means that the choice has to be made either to continue as before, but with ever greater potential for creating disaster, or to choose an alternative way forward and an acceptance of the fundamental realities of life lived out and expounded in Jesus' life and teaching. Humanity will be very reluctant to take this step into new territory, but it must be taken if the disasters threatened by the old way are to be overcome.

Jesus' teaching is widely perceived as idealistic but impractical, unable to match up to the real demands of life in the market place, the corridors of power and the street, and its practice is consequently only fleetingly in evidence, even in so-called Christian contexts. Alternatively it is treated as applying only to some other life outside this world. In practice, like other religious systems, attainment of this other life is often seen to require adherence to rules in some, rather limited, aspects of personal conduct but to have little wider application to the whole sphere of human activity. A further consequence is that Jesus' teaching is widely held to be prohibitive and joyless, denying enjoyment of the good things of life. This is ironic as he was criticised by his enemies for enjoying just those things and he spoke out against just those aspects of human behaviour which reduce the joy of life.

Our case, therefore, will be that Jesus' teaching sets out a practical way for all humans to develop beyond their current inadequate and unsatisfying state to one where their full potential can be realised and full satisfaction achieved. It is, we argue, the only way to survival and fulfilment and the major developments in the last 50 years in economics, science, politics and so forth have made it increasingly clear that "the acquisitive society" has no future. Cooperation is essential and we can see now more clearly the truth and

A Different Approach

power of what Jesus was saying. He was talking to ordinary people about the ordinary things of their lives and how these might be changed, but his teaching became tied into religious and otherworldly themes and needs to be detached from these again in order to understand its full implications. The teaching has radical implications for the whole of human life and its implementation would revolutionise business and economics, politics and international relations, science and social relations. It was not designed to demarcate who would and who would not achieve some special state of paradise after death (more of that later) but to establish here and now a good life for all. Far from being joyless, the new state on earth would provide joy and peace for all of a much more lasting kind than those briefer pleasures which Christians are often thought to prohibit (though in fact the only pleasures Jesus frowned on were those that damaged others or those who practised them).

Jesus did not lay down a body of directions for his followers on how to live their lives. In fact his only direct commands were that they should love God and love their fellow human beings and be ready to learn from the Holy Spirit who would guide their further understanding of Jesus' teaching. They were not asked to struggle to achieve some state of perfection for themselves by following certain set procedures, but to turn outwards, realise the crucial importance of relations with others in the well-being of each individual and focus always and only on the needs of these others. In addition he urged on them that they should be open to seeing things in a very different way from the prevailing viewpoint and not rush into judgement of others on the basis of existing prejudices. Of course human views are always open to change, but rarely in the radical way envisaged by Jesus. For him, it is as if the human brain has evolved to the point where it is no longer to be constrained by the old in-built desires and prejudices, but is now capable of a major shift to a new plane of understanding. From this all-embracing principle of love, which is present in most religions but not the core of them as it is of Jesus' teaching, a whole new way of life can be fashioned. There are no specific rules, because such rules are so often arbitrary, limited by time and culture and current knowledge, and destructively divisive.

Conforming to the law breeds self-righteousness, as he illustrated by the parable of the Pharisee who thanked God in his prayers that he was different from the unrighteous, while the tax collector expressed remorse for his sins and was, said Jesus, justified before God (Luke 18, 9ff.). For Jesus, God does not draw boundaries, based on insubstantial differences, but is a creator who aims high for the whole creation. The working out of the new principle is demonstrated, not in a series of directives, but in demonstrations and in graphic images of the nature of the new life. The Sermon on the Mount, including the Beatitudes (Matthew 5, 1ff.), the best-known collection of teaching in the New Testament, is not a series of rules, but offers general principles and describes the nature of those who will be blessed for living in the new way, then offers startling illustrations that simply keeping the supposed rules does not match up to what is needed. A fundamental change in viewpoint is needed, which for Jesus requires a change in notions about God and acceptance of God's creative love, which can bring about this change in us.

It is noticeable that the prevailing tenor of this teaching is not so much to condemn the "obvious" personal sins of murder, adultery, deceit and revenge, but to make the point that it is the underlying motives and attitudes that lead to these kinds of actions which need to be addressed. Simply doing the right thing through conforming to the law or through fear, though a starting point, will not in itself produce a revolution in human life. While the Christian churches have in theory been well aware of this fundamental teaching, in practice the message which comes across is that there are certain things that a Christian believer should not do. The emphasis has always been on what should not be done, rather than what positive principles should be followed. There is a fixed system for confession in many Christian traditions, but not a parallel fixed system for making promises of positive action. Negatives are easier to enforce. Hence there is a persistent focus on personal sexual behaviour, dishonesty and violence, and encouragement that Christians should generally be "nice" to others, and that about sums up the requirements. Also the emphasis has always been on individual relations with others and there is far less attention to the implications of Christ's teaching for the way the world organises the big policies which have far wider effects on the lives of millions than an individual's niceness or otherwise to immediate neighbours.

This change in emphasis from the original teaching is already apparent in the writings of Paul, who is prone to produce lists of sins and urge his readers to obey the authorities. He stresses that all are equal within the Church, but has little to say about changing the world outside. Ironically those with the power in "western" societies are more likely to be church attenders than those without (compare the congregations in suburbia and the inner city any Sunday), yet business, finance and politics are so often run as though Jesus had nothing to say about them and their effects on people. For many, religion seems to be a social event and a purely personal matter concerned with some notion of individual salvation, rather than the key to life and how to live it. While personal relations are the foundations of human life, in our day it is the decisions in boardrooms and cabinets, by bankers and politicians and scientists, that will decide whether humanity continues on its individualistic, violent, struggling way (or indeed whether it continues at all) or can move toward the better way which Jesus advocated. Consequently, our discussion of the urgent relevance of Jesus' teaching for the contemporary world will continue to concentrate on the big issues, where we see its application is most desperately needed and where a change from selfishness to love as the ruling principle would have the biggest effects. This is where we see the core of Jesus' message.

In the account in Chapter 3 of the Fourth Gospel (John 3, 1–12, see below) of Jesus' encounter with Nicodemus, we see this idea of new priorities expounded by Jesus, apparently to the confusion of Nicodemus. Nicodemus, one of the Jewish leaders,[1] was impressed by Jesus' ability to heal the sick, and came secretly at night (obviously afraid to be seen having anything to do with Jesus) to try and

---

1. The Fourth Gospel often refers to "the Jews" to indicate the religious leaders of the nation, but sometimes it clearly refers to the whole people. We have varied the translation accordingly.

discover more about him. He acknowledges that Jesus must be "from God" in view of what he is doing. Jesus asserts that no human being can make such judgements adequately ("see the kingdom of God") unless he has entered into a new state ("is born anew"). This new state requires action by "the Spirit" to make a person complete and able to understand clearly the truth about the creation and how it is intended to function. The gift of the Spirit gives a new freedom to range widely and freely in understanding and enquiry. Jesus implies that Nicodemus is limited in his understanding to the level granted by the normal physical process of birth, and though he is a great teacher, he has not got beyond this stage. But Jesus does have this extra perception and knowledge and can teach about the ways in which God works and the psychology of human beings (see the end of Chapter 2 of this Gospel: "needing no-one to demonstrate to him what human nature is").

John 3, 1–12[2]

One of the Pharisees named Nicodemus, a leader of the Jews, came to him under cover of night and said to him, "Rabbi, we know that you have come as a teacher from God, for no-one can perform the signs which you perform unless God is with him." Jesus answered him and said, "Assuredly I say to you that unless a person is born from above, he cannot see the kingdom of God." Nicodemus said to him, "How can a man be born when he is old? Surely he can't enter into his mother's womb a second time and be born?" Jesus answered, "Assuredly I say to you, unless anyone is born from water and spirit, he cannot enter into the kingdom of God. What is born from the flesh is flesh, and what is born from the spirit is spirit. Don't be amazed that I say to you, 'Everyone must be born anew.' The spirit breathes where it wishes and you hear its voice, but you don't know where it is coming from and where it is going. Everything born of the spirit is like this." Nicodemus answered him, "How can these things be?" Jesus answered, "You're a teacher of Israel and you don't know this? Assuredly I say to you that we are talking about what we know and witnessing to what we have seen and you don't accept our witness. If I speak to you people about earthly things and you don't believe, how will you believe if I speak to you about heavenly things?"

Psychologically there is nothing necessarily mystical about the proposed process, which is simply an enlargement of understanding which enables new ways of seeing life on earth and taking a wider perspective than the self-centred one commonly adopted. Human beings already pass through stages of understanding which develop new interpretations of what they see or hear (in the sense of what the neural apparatus of their visual or auditory system records and extracts), and these interpretations take account of a wider spectrum of information and experience. So babies come to see sequences as causal, objects as permanent, facial expressions as indicating anger and so on. Later in life men running about becomes a critical football match, marks on a page are an epic work of literature, interpretations beyond the grasp of even the higher apes. Any event can be understood at many different levels and in many different ways, depending on our previous experience and how the basic physical information that is delivered to the senses is encoded. What is more, one way of interpreting experience can preclude another more creative one.

What could be more plausible, then, than the possibility that there is more to be understood than our brains have yet achieved, a pattern in things which we have not yet picked up or have wilfully disregarded, forces we cannot yet measure, if we can be persuaded

2. The Gospel translations are by the authors from: *Nestle-Aland Greek–English New Testament* (eighth revised edition, 1998, 27th edition of Novum Testamentum Graece), Stuttgart: Deutsche Bibelgesellschaft.

to break out of the ways in which we have been conditioned by our past, so that whole new experiences may lie ahead? New discoveries are helping us to see things in new ways all the time. In recent years, albeit too slowly, we have gradually begun to see the earth and nature as a complex interconnected system, where interference in one area can have repercussions in other quite different ones, whereas previously and even now in many cases, nature is seen as a resource to be plundered without any wider effects. But new knowledge can be used for good or ill and the critical issue is whether we can learn to use it in creative and not in destructive ways, and can see it as a resource to benefit all rather than a source of gain for a few.

We should stress here that the process of being "born again" which Jesus recommends to Nicodemus has, in our view, nothing whatsoever in common with the widespread use of that term (which occurs only here in the Gospels) among certain groups of Christians, especially those professing the "fundamentalist" Christianity which is becoming so powerful in the USA. To our eyes, the term when used in that way has become relatively meaningless, signalling a claim to some type of emotional experience which seems to have little impact in moving the individual concerned toward an attitude such as Jesus recommended. Born-again Christians seem all too ready to judge, demonstrate hostility and divisive attitudes toward fellow humans, to seek power and to be ready to acquire wealth and use it to manipulate others to their own ends. We see little relation between this and the urging of Jesus to see and act in a new way.

The story of Nicodemus indicates the potential for a significant change in human understanding, but this requires a humility to see where we now stand, what our limitations are and the potential we have. Jesus does not offer a series of certainties or truths neatly packaged but an opening out to an uncertain future of further development, rather like evolution in fact, which never achieves a stable state but always generates change. Jesus has this understanding of the future because he is linked so closely to God, so he can offer to human beings the way to similar understanding here on the physical earth if they are willing to explore it. It is not just some future state in another world that he is offering but the possibility of a change here and now which will have implications for such a future state. The change is essential if the current concerns that prevail among humans are to be discarded and replaced with a fundamental drive to discover the truth which will necessarily involve developing a primary concern for others. This will "free up" our brains to range more widely and to understand differently, unbiased by short-term self-interest.

John 6; 1–15, 25–29

After this Jesus went away beyond the Sea of Galilee, the Sea of Tiberias. But a great crowd followed him, because they had seen the signs which he was doing on those who were sick. Jesus went up the mountain and sat down there with his disciples. It was near to the Passover, the Jewish Festival.

Jesus looked up and saw that a great crowd had come to him, so he said to Philip, "Where shall we buy bread so that these people can eat?" He said this to test Philip, for he himself knew what he intended to do. Philip answered, "Two hundred denarii worth of bread would not be enough for each of them to eat a little." Andrew, the brother of Simon Peter, one of his disciples, said to Jesus, "There is a young boy here who has five barley loaves and two fish, but what is that for so many people?" Jesus said, "Make the people sit down." There was a lot of grass in that spot. The men were about 5000 in number. Jesus took the loaves and gave thanks, then gave them to the seated people and likewise some of the fish, as much as they wanted. And when they were full, he said to his disciples, "Gather up the abundant fragments, so that nothing is lost." And they gathered them up and filled twelve baskets with fragments left from the five barley loaves by those who had eaten. When the people saw the sign which he had done, they said that this was truly the prophet who was to come into the world. Jesus therefore, knowing that they were going to come and seize him in order to make him king, went up again into the mountain on his own.

***

When they found him on the other side of the sea, they said to him, "Rabbi, when did you come here?" Jesus answered them, "Assuredly I say to you, you are looking for me not because you saw signs, but because you ate from the loaves and were satisfied. Don't work for bread that decays, but for the bread that remains till the life of eternity. The son of man will give you this life. God the Father has set his sign upon him." They said to Jesus, "What can we do in order to work God's work?" Jesus answered them, "This is God's work, that you believe in the one whom he sent."

The story of the feeding of the 5000 (John 6; 1–15, 25–29) again illustrates Jesus' efforts to open up human minds beyond their concerns for daily survival and pleasure. This story is common to all the gospels, but in the account in the Fourth Gospel several details are given that are absent elsewhere, suggesting it relies on someone who was present. Jesus asks Philip about the availability of bread and Philip is sceptical. Andrew, Peter's brother, contributes the information about loaves and fishes. Exactly what happened we can never know for certain – one possibility is that others produced food that they had brought once the example was given, thus breaking the habit of looking after themselves only and creating a psychological miracle, a sign of how the new life should operate.

But the main point of the story, and the follow-up the next day, is that Jesus again draws a distinction between physical and "spiritual" nourishment, and claims that he can provide the latter and that the latter is what humans need most. He saw the people's narrow focus on their physical needs and willingness to make him into a leader because he seemed able to supply these, but he knew that such a focus is the root of many problems and no way to real satisfaction and that leadership that responds to this type of demand is a recipe for failure and later disaster. We can see parallels in many an election campaign which focusses on promises of reduced taxation or material improvements, most often for those whose votes are crucial rather than for those who need them most, and ignores the bigger issues, such as which group in a society or the world at large is in the greatest need and what the most deep-seated needs of people and sources of conflict really are. Short-sightedness of this kind, in an effort to keep local taxes down, encouraged the sale of school playing fields in Britain in the 1980s, reducing opportunities for physical activity and challenge. Clearly young males, in particular, need such activity and, if frustrated by its absence, will turn to other ways of venting their energy, often anti-social ones. Yet the current "wave" of youth crime is not widely recognised as in any way connected with past political manoeuvring. On the wider front, there is an almost pathological unwillingness to admit links between world terrorism and frustration induced by the policies of the rich world designed to pander to selfishness in their own electorate. Jesus urges the people, in highly evocative language, to absorb the insights that he had to offer, which would provide so much more. Again a complete change of focus is urged, the consequences of which could be enormous.

There is nothing in Jesus' words after the people have been fed about doing the right thing or commands from God about what God wants, just a pleading to see things differently. Though he teaches with authority, he does not "lay down the law" and threaten punishment for those who fail to keep it. This is certainly different from a standard religious message and has little to do with living a "holy life" in the conventional sense. It won't produce a standard type of "good person". Each of us differs in capacity and potential and could develop much more if we were less bogged down by trying to gain things for ourselves and advance ourselves in the world's eyes. Jesus comes across as a live, creative and unceasingly aware person who pours out energy on behalf of others and longs for them to respond, rather than a good, safe advocate of right behaviour and conventional views about success in the world.

The point is made in a different way in an observation about the eye, which Jesus asserts is the "lamp" of the body (Matthew 6, 22; Luke 12, 34). If the eye (we might perhaps prefer to use the word "mind") is sincere in its regard, then the body will be full of light, which will in turn affect the whole behaviour of the body. If, on the other hand, the eye is devious in its regard, then the body will be full of darkness. The relevance of this observation can easily be seen in the context of family relationships and in attitudes to local community, national and international issues. If life is viewed from a narrow or fixed viewpoint (for example that all asylum seekers are cheats, everyone is out for their own interest, the innocent are fair game, all workers are idlers) then the whole of human life is distorted.

In the Beatitudes Jesus presented a set of dramatic illustrations of how life will look under the new viewpoint. These are included in both Matthew's and Luke's gospels. However, only Matthew has a more extended Sermon on the Mount which develops many of the themes further. The tenor of the Beatitudes differs somewhat in the Matthew and Luke versions, with Matthew's "blessed" (or "happy" or "rich" – note the implication of a close relation between these notions in popular thinking) person being more completely different from the normal human judgement of that condition than Luke's. For example Matthew's happy individual hungers and thirsts for justice (or righteousness), while Luke's merely hungers and will be satisfied. Matthew's poor in spirit are merely poor for Luke. The whole "topsy-turvy" nature of the exhortations in the Sermon on the Mount which follows seems more compatible with Matthew's approach than with Luke's and we therefore concentrate on the former (Matthew 5, 1–10). The familiarity of the words tends to obscure their radicalism.

Matthew 5, 1–10

Happy are the poor in spirit, for theirs is the kingdom of the heavens.

Happy those who mourn, for they shall be comforted.

Happy the gentle, for they shall inherit the earth.

Happy those that hunger and thirst for righteousness, for they shall be satisfied.

Happy those that show mercy, for mercy shall be shown to them.

Happy the pure in heart, for they shall see God.

Happy the peacemakers, for they shall be called sons of God.

Happy those that have been persecuted for righteousness; theirs is the kingdom of the heavens.

"Happy are the poor in spirit, for theirs is the kingdom of the heavens." The word traditionally translated as "blessed", as already indicated, also conveys ideas of happiness and riches, which are conventionally seen as closely related. The word for "poor" originally meant "beggars". So the world's standards for being at the top are reversed. In the divine scheme of things it is lack of conceit about one's own value that counts. Priority is given to the other person. If such an attitude prevailed, politics, advertising and academic activity, to name but a few contexts, would be drastically changed, we suggest for the better. Spin, exaggeration, denigration of the opposition, should give way to honest presentation and respect for others' views and a focus on the truth rather than sensation. The problems and injustices we have highlighted in Chapter 2 above would largely vanish. The humble do not compete for wealth and power and the more common this change of attitude the less need for such competition would become. The humble do not despise those who differ from them, so many sources of division and conflict would vanish. They do not consider their own desires should prevail over those of others. Because they consider others as of equal or greater worth than themselves, they will consider the needs of others rather than their own. Union Carbide would compensate its victims, drugs multinationals would make their products available where suffering required them, debt would not be used to manipulate whole nations and taxation would be rightfully regarded as a sharing among all because all are worthy. In personal relations too, conflict should give way to seeking consensus in the interests of all. No wonder such a change of heart is promised to produce a miraculous change in the whole of life.

The kingdom of God, or the kingdom of the heavens as Matthew has it, is referred to much more often in the first three gospels than in the Fourth Gospel. There has been argument over the years as to the precise meaning of this term, but there is much to suggest it has a particular appropriateness in relation to the next stage of evolution to which we have been referring. The overwhelming significance of the kingdom, its capacity to grow, the need to be ready for its coming, the distractions that can divert us from it, the different kind of outlook needed to become part of it, the change in priorities it calls for, are just some of the aspects which are reflected in brief sayings and longer parables. It is more a question of a way of life than a place. Indeed, it is life in accordance with the creative love of God.

"Happy those who mourn, for they shall be comforted." Again a startling juxtaposition. "Mourn" is misleading as it is associated in English with grieving for the dead, but the word refers to being sad in a more general sense. The word for comfort is the same as that used to refer to the Holy Spirit in the Fourth Gospel (which can be translated as Adviser, Counsellor and so on). So the words could convey the notion that those who find life discouraging will be given strength to see it differently and do something about it. Victory will not always be to the powerful in the world's sense.

"Happy the gentle, for they shall inherit the earth." It is not power as humanly conceived that will count in the new order of things, but being unassuming, gentle, considerate. Asserting the superiority of one's own religion or claiming a divine right to a country are strongly at variance with this assertion. The point of the first Beatitude is further reinforced.

A Different Approach

"Happy those that hunger and thirst for righteousness." Not, it should be noted, for earthly food. The Greek word and the English equivalent "righteousness" have unfortunate connotations, being associated with self-righteousness and public manifestation of being upright. For a Jew this consisted of living a personal life governed by the law and the same sense has tended to survive in Christianity. The Greek word, however, originally meant "justice", which can only be exercised in relation to others and the reference to hungering and thirsting stresses the need for constant urgent search rather than the self-satisfied assurance that one has matched up to the rules already. Strive for justice between all and the reward will be rich.

"Happy those that show mercy, for mercy shall be shown to them." Forgiveness will be reciprocated. Revenge is a self-perpetuating cycle (see Israel today) leading to mutual destruction. As Gandhi said, an eye for an eye leaves the world blind. The words are relevant to issues of debt, the administration of justice and the way we cope with anger. Elsewhere, when asked how often we should forgive, Jesus said seventy times seven, an uncountable number of times (Matthew 18, 21).

"Happy the pure in heart, for they shall see God." The word for "pure" originally meant clean in a physical sense, extended to a ritualistic one. The emphasis here is that it is not ritualistic purity that matters, but purity in thought and behaviour. This too, has commonly been interpreted in a very narrow sense, especially sexual, ignoring the potential of many other human actions and desires to destroy an individual, whether oneself or others.

"Happy the peacemakers, for they shall be called sons of God." Forgiveness again, but peacemaking is something more, requiring the vision and patience to see how a situation can be saved from degenerating into violence.

"Happy those that have been persecuted for righteousness; theirs is the kingdom of the heavens." "For righteousness" is not entirely clear. It means "on account of their righteousness", but see earlier for the implications of this word.

The overall picture conveyed is that a total change in priorities would benefit all and create a rich and happy world. The message is of hope that things can change in the new age. The injustices and inadequacies and unhappiness of the current human condition can be done away with if Jesus' message is acted on. Again we suggest that it is as if Jesus was pointing to the possibility of a further step in human evolution to achieve a new and richer existence. Now that evolution has reached a certain point, where consciousness, choice and understanding are possible, new possibilities for further change open up. This is how we are to discover the meaning of our existence. He presented a challenge to the current assumptions about how life should proceed, which can be taken up and tested like a scientific hypothesis. Like any testing process, this requires flexibility and search, not rigid adherence to fixed rules. Though other thinkers have made not dissimilar claims about the need for a change in human behaviour, Jesus' version was more radical and pervasive.

Attitude toward others

As is clear from much of the above discussion, the new way of living that Jesus advocates involves totally new priorities, compared with the prevailing human tendencies to compete and strive to acquire possessions and power. The emphasis, as we have frequently pointed out, is on better ways of living with each other on earth, rather than some magic translation to another life in the sky. The Lord's Prayer states, "Thy will be done, as in heaven, so on earth". So the better way of living needs to be implemented on earth, rather than our waiting around till we can enjoy it in heaven. This is summed up in Jesus' new commandment to the disciples (John 13, 31–35) to love one another as he has loved us. Though this was directed originally at the small group around him, it clearly applies to all who claim to be disciples of his. Moreover Jesus clearly demonstrated that his love was not restricted to those who claimed to be his followers, by his willingness to talk to and heal all sorts of people who were regarded as outside respectable society, such as lepers, tax collectors, Samaritans and so on.

John 13, 31–35

So, when he had gone out, Jesus said, "Now the son of man has been glorified and God has been glorified in him. And will glorify him in himself and will do this straight away. Little children, I will be with you for a little while yet. You will look for me and as I said to the Jewish leaders, 'You will not be able to go where I am going'. I now say this to you. I give you a new command, that you love each other, just as I have loved you so that you will love each other. In this way, everyone will know that you are disciples of mine, if you have such love among you."

One way in which he particularly demonstrated that he set up no barriers was in his attitudes to women and children, both regarded as of little account in a men's world. Even today in many cultures this is still true and Britain, a supposed example of civilised Christian society, has recently been castigated for its unacceptable treatment of some of its most vulnerable children in a report of the Children's Rights Alliance (*The Guardian*, 9 October 2003). Though the accounts we have do not report any formally appointed women disciples, there were certainly many close friends and followers of Jesus who were women. In fact the 12 disciples may not have been a specially accredited group, since the lists of names we have are not consistent, but may represent the Church's attempt to tie itself to Jewish history, with its twelve tribes. Also the records were written by men, tradition demanded 12 men, so 12 men it became. Apart from this there are many indications that Jesus treated women as equally worthy of his attention (the Samaritan woman discussed in the next chapter, the Phoenician woman in Matthew 15, 27, whose daughter he healed, Mary Magdalene, Martha and Mary). In one visit to the house of Martha and Mary, sisters of Lazarus (Luke 10, 38ff.), Jesus showed that he did not restrict women to domestic duties. Martha complained that her sister was not helping with the meal and Jesus firmly stated that in listening to his teaching Mary was focussing on the more important things in life.

Equally Jesus had a special attitude to children. When the disciples regarded women bringing their children to him as simply a nuisance (Matthew 19, 13), he firmly rebuked the disciples and welcomed the children. Asked who was the greatest in the kingdom of the heavens, he drew a child to him and said, "Truly, I say to you, unless you turn around and become like children, you will never enter the kingdom of the heavens" (Matthew 18, 3, also Mark 10, 15 and Luke 18, 17). It was the child's humility to which he was referring, as is clear from what follows. He was obviously aware that children could also be simply childish, but the care of children was of the greatest importance. Nothing should be done to cause them to stumble. If a child does not experience what it means to be valued, does not know love and respect and is not encouraged also to feel love and respect toward others, then indeed the likelihood is great that he or she will stumble in one way or the other and, moreover, will in turn produce children who are neither loved nor respected. This "cycle of deprivation" is not, of course, either inevitable or due entirely to the deficiencies of the parents, and could certainly be ameliorated, and probably eventually broken, by a greater concern for each other implemented in both structural and individual action to support those who need assistance of all kinds to help them cope with life.

Wealth

Jesus urged his listeners (Matthew 6, 21; Luke 12, 33) not to store up earthly treasures that are subject to moth and rust and attract thieves, but rather to store up those of greater importance, which are not vulnerable to the same threats. The reason for this piece of advice is, as he observes, that where one's treasure is there also one's

A Different Approach

heart is. He does not dwell on the consequences of such a focus but the ensuing 2000 years has given us ample opportunity to see just what happens when the heart is set on things that are transient and we have given some examples of the wider consequences above.

He also comments on our inability to serve two masters (Matthew 6, 24; Luke 16, 13). We either love the one and hate the other or vice versa, says Jesus. The two on which he focusses are God and material wealth, often rendered simply as "money". The question is essentially one of priorities, since there will obviously be some form of wealth, on however minimal a scale, in any human society. If concern for wealth is dominant then the demands of the creative love of God will fall on deaf ears or at most be seen as a tiresome factor to receive an occasional nod through good works, such as supporting charities and possibly attendance at church as part of an outward semblance of shared allegiance. To do good to "the poor" or assist this or that charity may seem worthy, but why are there poor or a need for charitable giving in the first place? Is there not some major deficiency present that suggests that the real implications of the creative love of God are not even considered seriously, never mind actually met. Indeed, Jesus observed at one point, almost wearily, "The poor you always have with you" (Mark 14, 7), being all too aware of the lack of disposition to do anything serious about that problem.

Another observation concerns the obsessive concern that existed then, and still does, for food and drink and clothes to wear. "Is not life more than food and the body more than clothing?" asks Jesus (Matthew 6, 25; Luke 12, 22ff.). He draws attention to the beauty of the flowers of the field, even when compared to the reputed splendour of Solomon, and the provision of food for the birds as just two examples of the provision built into God's overall concern for the world. We know now how much we have imperilled the birds by our human activities and we are aware of the natural beauty of wildlife, when not despoiled by human intervention, and we can admire the beauty we can help to create by careful cultivation. But we can be distracted from most other considerations by the "needs" for food and clothing and we are at our most vulnerable when pursued by those who seek to make money out of these obsessions. Jesus suggests that we have got it the wrong way round. If concern for the implications of the creative love of God for all mankind were uppermost in our minds, then, in the process of pursuing this concern we could discover ways in which the basic needs of all could be met without each pursuing his or her own ends obsessively. And, we might add, in which the creation was not despoiled in the acquisitive drive of humanity.

It would, of course, necessitate a new economic system, but the present one is not the boon for all which its advocates claim. It does not bring peace of mind and relief from stress, whether such stress arises from attempts to overachieve or from the closure of industries, disruption of communities and consistent experience of underachieving. Indeed it cannot be claimed to lead to peace rather than war, either on the battlefields of economic competition often in a stark and brutal form, as for instance in the assault to sell Genetically Modified Foods to those who regard them with suspicion, or on the actual battlefields of military strife. We have come some way toward the concept of getting together globally to reduce the risk of open warfare and a majority of nations has accepted the possibility of putting on trial those who involve themselves in perpetrating genocide. Could we ever get to the point where we get together globally to monitor economic exploitation and take active steps against it? This would mean a huge step beyond the present international meetings of the rich for their own advantage, which bring minimal, if any, advantage to the poor.

Some 2000 years later we can look back at the advice that Jesus gave about money and see something of what is involved in ignoring it. Of course there are other facets of life, of which he was equally aware. So long as money, and what it buys, remains at the centre of things and possession of it is valued as it is, then there will inevitably be a tendency to look down on those who do not have it. This can lead in turn to increasing levels of distrust in society and to an intelligible desire on the part of the despised to get even in some way.

Jesus returned frequently to this theme of wealth and possessions. It is not that physical things are in themselves evil. After all we live in a physical world, created by God, and Jesus himself certainly enjoyed

A Different Approach

a good meal. At one point he commented on the fickleness of people, comparing the reaction to John the Baptist's austerity ("He is deranged") and to himself ("Look, a glutton and a drunkard, a friend of tax collectors and sinners!" Matthew 11, 19). But excessive focus on such things distorts and narrows the vision, and often involves exploitation of others. Jesus challenged the rich man who offered to follow him to sell his possessions as a sign of his new priorities, but the man could not take the plunge (Mark 10, 17–27). "It's easier for a camel to pass through the eye of a needle than for a rich man to enter the kingdom of God" was Jesus' comment (Matthew 19, 23). (Even if the "needle" is taken, as by many authorities, to refer to a narrow gate in Jerusalem, the point is clear.) However, he goes on to point out that it is not impossible, just difficult. The disciples are surprised, presumably because wealth was regarded as a sign of God's favour. By implication, Jesus denies this crude assumption that gods are there to promote the physical comforts of their followers.

Mark 10, 17–27

And as he was setting out on his journey, a man ran up and knelt down and asked him, "Good teacher, what shall I do to inherit life to eternity?" Jesus said to him, "Why do you call me good. No-one is good except God. You know the commandments. 'Don't kill, don't commit adultery, don't steal, don't give false evidence, don't rob, honour your father and mother.'" But the man said, "Teacher, I have observed all these from my youth." But Jesus looked at him and loved him and said, "One thing is missing. Go, sell everything you have and give the proceeds to the poor, and you will have treasure in heaven, and come here and follow me." But he was shocked at these words and went away grieving, for he was a man with many possessions.

And Jesus looked around and said to his disciples, "How difficult it will be for those with wealth to go into the kingdom of God." The disciples were amazed at his words, but Jesus said again to them, "Children, how difficult it is to enter the kingdom of God. It's easier for a camel to pass through the eye of a needle than for a rich man to enter the kingdom of God." But they were deeply astonished and said to each other, "And who can be saved?" Jesus looked at them and said, "With men it's impossible, but not with God, for everything is possible with God."

However, this passage is too readily taken as a total condemnation of possessions. John Wesley insisted that he must retain only a small proportion of his earnings and could justifiably be called a robber if he left anything after his death. Others have taken the vow of poverty and retired into a separated community which ironically often ended up wealthy through endowments, gifts and its own frugality. However, Jesus is clearly addressing an individual case when he challenges this man, who has asked what is lacking in his life. It is, says Jesus, your wealth which is preoccupying you (for others it might have been fame or power). There is no indication that the man was using his wealth for any particularly good purpose other than keeping himself comfortable and safe, and that is the problem. Jesus implies that keeping the law, however assiduously, is inadequate, when the basic priorities are weak. But possessions are not necessarily bad. Elsewhere the tax collector Zacchaeus was commended when he promised to give away only half his possessions, even though they had been acquired by dubious means. The home of Lazarus and his sisters seems to have been a comfortable haven where Jesus was happy to rest from time to time. What Jesus objects to is the tendency for wealth and its pursuit to dominate life – "You cannot serve God and money". Where the pursuit of wealth is the dominant concern, those who pursue it will put their own interests first, to the impoverishment, neglect and disempowerment of others. And inequality of wealth generates inequalities in many other things

A Different Approach

such as access to decent housing, education, health care and security. Ironically church attendance is higher among the more affluent, very many of whom regularly vote for policies designed to perpetuate their advantages.

Nor is Jesus suggesting that the life of poverty is a calling for a small select group of followers. He is addressing a big crowd. What he has to say applies to all and what he says is that pursuing wealth for oneself, however good the intentions, is not a recipe for bringing about the good of all. In fact quite the reverse will occur. But if we could all put others first and give their needs priority, no-one would lack for the necessities, or indeed the comforts of life.

Frequently in our day those with riches are presented in the media as estimable achievers who have shown enterprise and created wealth, done their bit for society and so forth. Their philanthropy is praised, even though it may be but a drop in their total riches or designed to achieve some other goal. Like the societies of the Old Testament and Jesus' contemporaries, our society sees wealth as a good, a just reward for virtue while the poor deserve their lot due to their ignorance and laziness (an example of how power justifies itself by denigrating the powerless). Jesus denies this. Moreover, individual wealth is rarely the result of providing great benefits to society. In the worst cases it is the result of lucky or dubious deals, often totally non-productive, manipulating the levers of power or finance for one's own benefit, cleverness rather than creativity. In recent years, electronic communications have fostered a huge international trade in currency. Vast sums are moved about the globe at the press of a button in the hope of making millions simply by movements in exchange rates. This has siphoned off resources which could have been used in the old-fashioned way as investments to generate production, employment and useful goods, particularly in the poorer areas of the world. And the acquisition of great wealth too often means gathering to oneself what might have been spread more widely (in higher wages for example), rather than provision of new or needed benefits to society. Such acquisition all too often becomes an end in itself, regardless of the value or consequences of what is needed to achieve it. Recently the multi-millionaire Nicholas van

Hoogstraten claimed that, "whatever money you have, it is never enough" and the case of the chief executive of GlaxoSmithKline has been referred to above. But material wealth has no ultimate value. As the popular saying goes, "You can't take it with you", and Jesus made the same point in the story of the rich man who built bigger barns and died the next day (Luke 12, 13ff.).

The same point applies to nations. The meanness of the rich nations has been discussed in detail earlier, and their policies designed to siphon off even more of the world's wealth to themselves. The consequences of these policies for the anger of the poor and the health of the planet are all too easy to foresee. Surveys show that above a certain relatively modest level (around $10,000 annual income per head; *The Guardian*, 17 April 2002) additional national wealth does not produce greater happiness. In fact it may reduce it because great national wealth often conceals huge differences within the nation, creating a discontented poor underclass lacking in basic necessities and fostering envy and dissatisfaction.

Power

Jesus denies that God works in the world by exercising power in the way that human leaders exercise it. This is shown in his own refusal to play the power game, demonstrated in the allegorical story of the Temptations (Luke 4, 1–13) and in the account of the Last Supper in the Fourth Gospel (John 13, 1–16). The latter includes a striking event which is absent in the other gospels, the washing of the disciples' feet. Again a contrast is drawn between physical and psychological or spiritual cleanliness. Peter protests, impetuous as usual, but Jesus says that the washing is needed as a sign that Peter is a disciple. Note the reversal – the leader does the menial act to confirm that they are his followers. And then he tries to explain that he is showing how they should treat each other. He is their Lord but this does not confer a special status on him as the world normally expects. He is set apart in his closeness and obedience to his father, but this does not exclude humility, a readiness to play the role of servant. He is turning upside down the usual notions of power, the status it brings and the authority over others. This is what they need to learn if they are to communicate the true meaning of authority (and give some insight into God's authority) to others. Human societies have never worked this way. The Church, which knows this truth in theory, has never operated with it in practice, but has created a hierarchy of authority and power.

Luke 4, 1–13

And Jesus, full of the Holy Spirit, turned back from the Jordan and was led in the spirit in the wilderness for forty days, being tempted by the devil. And he ate nothing during those days and at the end he was hungry. The devil said to him, "If you are the son of God, speak to this stone so that it becomes bread." And Jesus answered him, "It is written that mankind will not live on bread alone."

And leading him up high, the devil showed him all the kingdoms of the inhabited world in an instant of time and said to him "I will give you all this authority and the glory of these kingdoms, because it has been handed over to me and I will give it to whoever I wish. Therefore, if you will bow down before me, all of it will be yours." And Jesus answered him, "It is written, 'You will bow down to the Lord God and you will worship only him.'"

He led him to Jerusalem and stood him on the very top of the temple and said to him, "If you are the son of God, throw yourself down from here, since it is written that, 'He will command his angels to guard you' and 'They will lift you up on their hands, so that you will not knock your foot on a stone.'" And Jesus answered him that it is written, "You shall not tempt the Lord your God."

And when the devil had completed all the temptations, he went away until another chance would come.

John 13, 1–16

Before the feast of the Passover, Jesus saw that his hour was come to go from this world to his Father. He had loved his own people in the world and loved them to the end. While they were having supper, the devil had already put it into the heart of Judas Iscariot, the son of Simon, to betray him. Jesus knew that the Father had put everything into his hands and that he had come from God and was going to God. He got up from supper and put off his clothes and took a towel and tied it round him. Then he poured water into the basin and began to wash the disciples' feet and wipe them with the towel that he had tied round him. So he came to Simon Peter, who said to him, "Master, are you going to wash my feet?" Jesus answered him, "What it is that I'm doing you don't know just now, but you will know after this." Peter said to him, "You won't ever wash my feet." Jesus said to him, "If I don't wash you, you will have no share with me." Simon Peter said to him, "Master, not only my feet but also my hands and head." Jesus said to him, "The one who is bathed has no need to wash any more than his feet, but is completely pure. And you are pure, but not all of you." For he knew who would betray him and for that reason he said that they were not all pure.

When therefore he had washed their feet and had taken up his clothes and lain down again, he said to them, "Do you know what I have done for you. You call me, 'teacher and master' and you speak well, for I am such. If therefore I, your master and teacher, have washed your feet, you too ought to wash each others' feet. I have given you an example so that you too will do what I have done for you."

This is Jesus' clearest statement about power. He is not just making a statement about outward humility but about the need for inward change. Power reaches into every human relationship and until it is seen for what it is in all its corrupting potential, abuse of it will continue to destroy people and societies. Yet Jesus claims that there is a way out of the power game because neither God nor he himself wants to exercise that kind of authority. He wants to release humans from both exercising and being subject to power. He does not want to be a king, either in a religious or a political sense. (Despite this the churches depend heavily on purveying the notion of a religious king.) His understanding of the normal interactions of human beings constantly suggests that power in all life, from the large scene to the small, would be very differently exercised should he be understood. There needs to be an ability to see what one is doing with power and what power is doing to oneself.

Recent experimental studies of the exercise of power (Lee-Chai and Bargh, 2001) have necessarily dealt with the exercise of power in small groups or between individuals rather than on a large scale, but have produced some interesting observations on the interrelations between personality, perception of others and the way in which power is exercised. Power is the ability to achieve desired outcomes, so we all try to attain and exercise some level of power and our own self-image is closely tied to our perception of our own ability to achieve such outcomes. Studies on the whole do not support the popular adage that "Power tends to corrupt" but rather suggest that the way power is exercised depends on the prior personality and attitudes of the individual. Hence power can be, and sometimes is, exercised altruistically. In this case it is clear that changing the basic motivations of people toward a greater consideration of others will in turn affect the way in which they exercise any power they possess. However, it likely that those who pursue power are just those individuals with a personality that has a tendency to be self-centred, and hence will be prone to develop increased tendencies of this nature when they acquire power. For this reason it is still essential that society devises methods of preventing abuse of power. Bargh and Alvarez (Chapter 3, ibid.) point to the success of consciousness-raising campaigns on civil and gender inequalities in bringing into awareness the rights of others and in highlighting the issue of unconscious and denied discrimination through presentation of carefully assembled evidence. They suggest that similar tendencies, which are often unconscious, to exercise power for self-interest and to deny and justify such biases by denigration of those who suffer from it, might also be reduced by exposure and evidence of the reality of the situation. However, ultimately, as in all else we have been saying, a fundamental change in human motivation and attitude toward power will be needed, and Jesus demonstrates the direction in which this needs to move. More study is needed of the way power and its use works in the human mind, how far this depends on in-built instincts and how far on upbringing. And how the way of the world can be changed into using power creatively and humbly for the benefit of others.

This need is apparent in human dealings with the natural world, no less than with each other. Jesus urged us to look at the lilies, be humble in the face of nature's glory and live in harmony with the workings of nature. Instead we, in the west at least, strive to dominate and use nature, and this misuse of power is catching up with us. Jesus demonstrates that power is entrusted to facilitate the growth and well-being of others and their fulfilment, not as a means to further one's own ends. Authority and power are to be exercised in service, not in ruling, and this change of attitude is needed in humans to achieve the better life. It is so easy for those in authority to rationalise their decisions and deceive themselves. Clever expressions are devised to conceal the real effect of decisions. Rarely do those who cause the suffering of others through their mistakes of judgement lack sufficient skill to avoid for themselves the crises and the consequences that fall on others. Frequently of late massive failure at the top has been rewarded with a massive payoff, while those at the bottom carry the can or the losses or both. The most striking recent example of this has been in the collapse of the giant American multinational Enron, where those in the know about the forthcoming disaster sold their shares profitably before the truth came out, leaving the majority of lesser shareholders with nothing. There is a gross misuse of power and the reappraisal of how authority can be operated justly for the good of all in every sphere is one of the most urgent requirements in human life. But would those in authority accept such a move, still less finance and support it?

The future

So, what of the future of humanity. Do we despair or is there some chance of change? Some commentators see the trend to inequality accelerating. William Rees-Mogg (*The Times*, 30 January 1997, quoted by David Jenkins, 2000) sees a new class developing which can manipulate the electronic technology to its own advantage. "It places a high value on consumer goods, on education, on fitness, on travel. It yearns for an uncertain spirituality. It also places a high value on personal excitement; if it is liable to be enslaved by anything, it is by the craving for stimulation, by the New Age cults, by drugs, by sex and by Hollywood. This class is coming to dominate modern civilisation." Jenkins also quotes a report by Larry Elliott from the 1997 World Economics forum at Davos (*The Guardian*, 3 February 1997): "Some US economists see the America of the future as having 20 percent of well-educated professionals earning $75,000 to $500,000 a year to carry out orders from the super-rich, while the remaining 80 percent that now have a median family income of $30,000 a year will do all the dirty work and see their living standards eroded year by year. In other words, a modern form of feudalism."

John Gray (2002, p. 187) is even more pessimistic, suggesting that "homo rapiens" is creating a world in which the replacement of humans by machines is inevitable and desirable and that these machines would eventually develop human-like characteristics of emotions and self-awareness. He also suggests that already so much human labour is now done by machines that large numbers of humans are becoming superfluous and that a new economy is evolving (designer religions, and illegal suppliers of drugs and sex) "to entertain and distract a population which – though it is busier than ever before – secretly suspects that it is useless" (ibid., p. 160). "Only the thrill of the forbidden can lighten the burden of a life of leisure" (ibid., p. 164). This would seem to be over-generalising the trends seen by Rees-Mogg and Elliott and turning a blind eye to the immense challenges facing humanity which we have persistently highlighted in the needs throughout the world which call for action. It is not that work is lacking, but that the motivation to undertake it succumbs to concern for the self. Gray's vision also implicitly assumes that humanity will continue to focus on the need of the individual in isolation rather than the vital importance of relations with others, which we have been stressing.

True, there is opposition to this society that has been constructed based on competition, power and violence, where satisfaction is measured by the possession of objects or some temporary new sensation. But it is intermittent, weak and unco-ordinated and barely noticed unless it adopts the same philosophies as the system it opposes, using violence to gain publicity. Such methods will never heal our damaged societies. History shows all too often how those with the best of intentions committed to the overthrow of evil systems become tainted in the struggle and if they achieve power, can end up with characteristics all too similar to those they vowed to remove. George Orwell described the process to perfection in *Animal Farm*.

So, do we despair? Are humans totally subject to their supposed genetic inheritance, unable to forego the urge to win, acquire, dominate? Is this obsession with possessions an inevitable part of human nature? Are they incapable of adopting any other way of life or even considering that it might work better? Does history demonstrate that cultural changes can never overcome these inevitable genetic tendencies? Is there any other way feasible? If we accept the view that creation and life are just accidents, governed by chance and survival of the fittest, and that the same processes continue to operate and underlie all that happens, it seems we have to accept that only minor amelioration of these inherited tendencies can ever be achieved. (Indeed on this view these problems are not really important as human beings are just complex machines with a short life.) However, checks and balances of opposed interests can perhaps be manipulated to reduce conflict. For the sake of greater security the rich may be persuaded to forego some benefits in order that the lot of the poor may be improved, though paradoxically it is in recent years in the most prosperous societies on earth that resistance to taxation has become a potent political force, ensuring the retention of individual wealth rather than its deployment in public services for the general good. There is little sign at present that greater wealth induces greater willingness to share and indeed no reason why it should if life is simply a struggle for survival of the fittest. Yet it is far from obvious that life with more money is necessarily more fulfilling. Happiness ratings do not continue to increase as national wealth goes on expanding beyond a certain point, as pointed out above. Something more radical is needed if change is to occur, a Big Bang in human psychology provoked by realising the futility and self-defeating nature of the present system. The present attitude is not completely inevitable. Human beings can change, and not all are driven by greed. When Britain was in the middle of a war and incomes were a fraction of what they now are, there was widespread support for the Beveridge Report's proposals that the whole community should adopt principles of mutual support, even from those who stood to lose from the policy.

At present those who try to counter the prevailing forces on which world commerce depends are fighting a brave, but marginal campaign to ameliorate the worst effects of capitalistic self-interest, but one only has to attend the AGM of a big company to realise the problem of introducing the smallest consideration into company policies other than the desire of shareholders for maximum profit at any cost, followed by a good free lunch (actually not that good!). Whether the investors depend for their returns on construction, biological engineering, oil or tobacco, to name just a few, even the mildest suggestion that the wider effects of the company's activities should be taken into account when planning the future developments and that the well-being of those affected by these policies should be an important factor in decision making is certain to be treated with contempt and disdain by the vast majority of those present. The system is not intended to foster such considerations and any attempt to introduce them is swept aside by the power of the corporate shareholders such as pension funds, even if a few individuals may be willing to give them a hearing. In any case, the corporate shareholders will all have registered their massive votes before the Annual General Meeting, without hearing any of the debate.

Occasionally minor restraints may be introduced by governments or even by companies themselves. Ethical policies have in recent years been promoted by the Co-operative Bank, for example, and Triodos Bank offers targeted investment in a number of areas on behalf of those in particular need or investment that pays special attention to environmental considerations. Methods of returning power in some small measure to the local level have been devised, such as local exchange trading schemes and time banks, whereby local groups trade among themselves in skills or time which they can offer each other independently of the monetary system. Another idea is to tax all currency speculation on international markets (the Tobin Tax) and use the proceeds for the benefit of the poor, but this has received short shrift from the international powers that control the financial system. The most effective sources of change are small local initiatives run by and for local people. In Argentina, a state bankrupted largely by the policies imposed by the International Monetary Fund and the greed of its ruling class, the collapse of the financial system has stimulated a vast network of local groups, co-operating to meet each other's needs, for example by trading directly in goods (see Naomi Klein, *The Guardian*, 25 January 2003). An international network of resistance to the power of global capital is slowly developing.

Several of these examples are effective because they exemplify methods of escaping from the tyranny of the world financial system. Douthwaite (1999) describes how the current system, quite apart from the ways we have already discussed in which it disempowers the poor, generates wealth out of (in effect) nothing for private banks who "create" money by credit and thereby drive the need for unsustainable economic growth to pay the interest on this credit. The system exists on a knife edge between inflation and recession – if we, the customers, stop spending, it will all fall apart. Douthwaite considers how an alternative system (or several parallel systems) could be devised which would not have this suicidal trend, would constrain the unsustainable consumption of limited resources and benefit trade at a local level and under local control.

In education, too, small examples of an alternative to the prevailing competitive ethos, both in the system and in the values imparted, can be found. Sterling (2001) discusses the need for "sustainable education", as an alternative to the view of education as a system to be managed for economic purposes. Sustainable education would take account of the increasing realisation that the whole world is complex and interdependent and that the different crises currently apparent are interconnected. "Without an ecological understanding, we are in real danger of creating post-modern learning institutions, whose graduates are able to exploit others and the environment more efficiently and effectively than their predecessors" (ibid., p. 45). (Compare the similar predictions of William Rees-Mogg and Larry Elliott above.) Sterling quotes a number of examples of educational initiatives to inculcate a different ethos, for example, the Small School in Devon (ibid., p. 69). This school,

> sets out to foster community, not individualism; simplicity rather than consumerism; spirituality rather than materialism. Smallness allows participation, positive relationships, and whole-school policies for environmental and social sustainability; an egalitarian pay structure, an ethical purchasing policy favouring organic, fair trade, local and recycled goods, a curriculum that includes practical skills like growing food and cooking, knowledge of global issues like climate change, fair trade and world debt, and values of spirituality through silence and a daily Peace Prayer. Natural materials are used in classrooms, and the grounds are managed for wildlife, without the use of chemicals.

Ultimately the world system can only be fundamentally changed when the principle of concern for others as a total way of life is accepted. If this were to operate as the basic principle instead of, as at present, each fighting for themselves, it is obvious that the examples we have cited (Union Carbide, asbestos, drug availability, avoidance of responsibility for harmful errors, the sufferings of the indebted, sale of arms, destruction of the natural resources on which we and future generations depend, growing inequality, ignoring the real sources of crime) would have very different outcomes. Indeed many of these problems would never have occurred if that principle had been operating. What we are trying to do here is to stress the fundamentals of the message put forward by Jesus, stripping away the confusing superstructure that has been erected upon his life and death and teaching, which all too often operates to destroy it. We are trying to show that it is realistic and applicable, not a lot of pious waffle about a future life, that it is intellectually tenable and emotionally deeply satisfying, and that without it humanity seems all too likely to perish in its own conceits. Simply to brush it aside as well-intentioned but unworkable is to act like the scientist who refuses to test an alternative hypothesis to a prevailing theory even when the theory is clearly not working well. Until we try them out, we cannot pronounce on the status of Jesus' proposals.

If more can be persuaded to test the hypothesis, more influence can be brought to bear to change the system. Initially this might take the form of small changes, encouraging firms to observe some ethical principles and to consider the effect of their operations on the future of the ecosystem on which our descendants will depend, to devote some resources to finding cures for tropical diseases which affect the poor but not the rich (and recently the risks of these diseases affecting even the rich have been pointed out, as for example the steady increase in tuberculosis in Britain in the last decade, including strains resistant to current antibiotics), to persuade governments to limit the sales of arms and to really cancel the debts which are crippling the poorest countries of the world. Perhaps the Jewish Jubilee should be revived and all debts cancelled every 50 years.

A Different Approach

A principle of not harming others by individual or corporate action would be a start, but only a start. The love shown by Jesus is positive, not simply restraining. The needs of others are the first consideration. Clearly if all were to operate on this principle, the inequalities and injustices which are such a feature of our world should disappear. The problem comes when some do operate on the principle and others do not. But Jesus stated and showed that even in this situation, love is stronger than selfishness. There is even some scientific evidence supporting the view that co-operation makes sense.

Dawkins (1989, pp.168 ff) summarises some studies by John Maynard Smith and others on how different strategies for life (competitive, co-operative, mixtures and so on) might contribute to the welfare of an imaginary species and be passed on down the generations. The process was simulated on a computer. Individuals were assumed to inherit a strategy, such as always fighting when conflict arose over a resource (hawks) or adopting a non-violent method for resolving the conflict (doves). Hawks will obviously always win so long as they encounter only doves and their genes will pass on more successfully to the next generation. But more hawks will be born and this means more fights, with the risks of defeat, damage and even death. So the balance tilts back and fewer hawks may be born. Eventually a balance is reached in the population, but this is not necessarily the most advantageous state for all, only the state which evolution would produce, given that set of circumstances. (Perhaps we are in something like that state now.)

However, Dawkins also points out elsewhere in the book (ibid., p. 201) that "We alone on earth [i.e. human beings] can rebel against the tyranny of the selfish replicators [i.e. genes]." Our ability to be aware in advance of consequences of our actions opens up the possibility of evaluating the best strategy for all, which is for all to behave as doves, and adopting it. It would also be necessary to devise methods of detecting and preventing the intrusion of the disruptive elements which would destroy this state and cause a return to a state under which all would be worse off in the long run. It may seem that Dawkins admission of the possibility of rebellion against the genetic inheritance is incompatible with his passionate advocacy of the all-determining power of the genes, but in an endnote (ibid., p. 331) he argues that this is not so. "We, that is our brains, are separate and independent enough from our genes to rebel against them." But this would seem to admit that the whole is something more than the sum of its parts, and that the combination has an ability not present in any single component or predictable from those components. In this case people are not just "survival machines" (Dawkins' term) built by genes. In fact Dawkins frequently acknowledges this, but equally he is fiercely opposed to acknowledging that there might be further implications of this admission. We will discuss the role of the genes and human freedom in more detail later.

Geras (1998, p. 57), writing from a different (but not fundamentally different) perspective from our own, asks a similar question to the one we are pursuing:

> Can one envisage a moral culture so transformed as to give real practical force to the sense of responsibility for the safety of others... Could one feasibly entertain the vision of a global human community in which an obligation to come to the assistance of others in danger or distress was widely felt as amongst the most powerful of imperatives, moving people to action when the risks of acting were small to non-existent, making a serious demand on their consciences – on their day-to-day deliberations – even when the risks were greater than that, and making of shame something more than a "metaphysical" shadow, more than a post hoc individual sentiment following failure to act; making of shame, and of the foretaste of it, an effective, mobilizing norm of social life?

He points out that what might be called the "liberal" outlook focusses on the notion of not harming others and that under such a perspective it is acceptable not to take personal responsibility for all the problems of others ("A liberal culture underwrites moral indifference;" p. 59). An alternative ethical view is that there is a duty of aid to others, but Geras argues that we must not be drawn into setting ourselves standards fit only for saints. He then explores some experiences of those within the extreme environment of the concentration camps, forced by the situation to put their own survival first, even when they felt a compulsion to help others, because their own destruction would remove even that small contribution. In the prevailing climate of our current society lesser parallels are apparent; the amount needing to be done for others is enormous and attempting to cope with every call can be self-destructive. If more accepted such a responsibility, the burden would decrease but, "How ... can one realistically conceive a path toward the state of affairs in which they will have become inclined to behave in that way? I do not have an answer to this question; no more than anyone else does, so far as I know" (ibid., p. 74).

This is, of course, a realist conclusion if one assumes that humanity has to pull itself up by its own fragile bootstraps, starting with only a metaphysical feeling that is frequently quite irrational. We might ask whence comes such a feeling? Though we may envisage similar changes and methods to those Geras would advocate, we are less pessimistic, since we are arguing that humanity has not reached an evolutionary stopping point, where the psychological ingredients remain stable and inadequate for the task. We will come in the next chapter to Jesus' confident assertion that he spoke for God and that God's purpose was to offer humanity the means to take a new step. It is difficult to see how, without such support, even the most fervent appeals for change can succeed, however practical and realistic they may seem. We will, however, argue that advice and support is waiting to be tapped, which can change human psychology and revolutionise those structures of our society which produce our present discontents.

A number of recent suggestions have been made about how humanity will have to change in order to survive, and offer interesting comparisons with those made by Jesus 2000 years ago. The World Resources Institute, a Washington-based environmental think-tank, has argued that to avoid the threats to humanity's future posed by our current lifestyle, and achieve a sustainable world, at least six changes are urgently needed: to a stable world population; to technology that has minimal impact on the environment; to an economy in which real costs are charged to users, including environmental costs to deter further loss of our limited natural resources; to a fairer income distribution; to united supranational planning; and to better communication, enabling the world's citizens to understand the challenges and hence agree on solutions. To get to such a situation will require "the renunciation or sublimation or transformation of our traditional appetites: to outbreed, outconsume and conquer our rivals, especially our rivals in other tribes" (Murray Gell-Man, quoted by Waldrop, 1994, pp. 350–351). It sounds familiar, though the emphasis is negative in contrast with the positive creative force of love advocated and offered by Jesus.

Sterling (2001, p. 75) quotes a survey of experts in nine countries on what characteristics will be needed to cope with likely major global trends in the new century. In order of importance there was a consensus on the following: looking at problems in a global context; working co-operatively and responsibly; accepting cultural differences; thinking in a critical and systematic way; solving conflicts non-violently; changing lifestyles to protect the environment; defending human rights, and participating in politics. The agreement between these two sets of suggestions is striking.

Barrow (1998, p. 142) has also described some speculations about how the future might evolve for a technologically sophisticated race such as human beings. One possibility is that a race of cerebral beings will emerge who learn to control their urge to expand and manipulate Nature, and, by halting their technological advance, will be able to live in equilibrium with their environment, including, of course, each other. Such a race would need to develop non-material goals and sophisticated altruistic and ethical principles. The alternative scenario envisaged is a rat race in which survival is a hard, and possibly ultimately unsuccessful, struggle.

The choice is on offer, if we believe that we are not puppets. With a change in motivation on all sides, however, certainly the present system could begin to look very different. With a new direction, nobody would wish to profit from products which harm others (tobacco, implements of torture, most armaments, to name but a few) or which are manufactured at the cost of the planet's future (dangerous chemicals, mahogany furniture, possibly genetically modified organisms) and resources would be directed to meeting need, differences in wealth would largely disappear, limits might be placed on the size and wealth of companies. And so forth. Ultimately, a different system for running the world needs to be developed. At present competitive capitalism is triumphant and earlier attempts to create other systems (which were assuredly in practice not based on love, whatever their ideals) have failed miserably.

Your reaction is likely to be that this is unrealistic utopianism. It is not utopianism, since we do not offer a blueprint but only highlight Jesus' plea for different principles and openness. In fact we will be arguing that this is God's will for his creation. Whether it is unrealistic nobody knows until the experiment is made. The views cited above suggest that it makes good sense. The key question is whether humans prefer to continue as now. You may so prefer, if you are doing nicely, thank you, but note the earlier points about the malaise of the wealthy world. If you are in the Gaza strip or the slums of Calcutta or some areas of large British cities, you may feel that the only answer is violent revolution, but you have no power and violence begets more violence. Perhaps instead, you might feel, as Gandhi said, when asked his view on Christian civilisation, that "it would be a good idea", ironically implying that the true version was very different from the existing version. Like Gandhi, we see little sign of any such thing at present, but we wish to clear the way for at least an effort toward such a new start.

Chapter 4
Jesus' God and His Purpose

We have attempted to show in the last chapter that the key aspects of Jesus' teaching have a very direct application to the needs of the world and to solving the problems that threaten the future of humanity. These teachings, he claimed, reflected the way God wanted humanity to develop and were designed to promote the ultimate divine purpose. The whole justification for the proposed new way of viewing life and the urge to put the needs of others first was that, in Jesus' view, God sees his creation in this way and all human beings are precious to him.

It might be argued, however, that the teachings make good sense, though admittedly difficult to implement in practice, simply from a practical worldly point of view, and that Jesus' constant references to God were just a reflection of the age in which he lived and the people to whom he spoke. In our own age, perhaps, this divine attribution is unnecessary and tends to discredit the teachings. After all, it might be claimed, science has shown that we are only the result of random permutations, that there is no purpose in creation and that invocation of a divine creator is unnecessary, even ridiculous. Moreover, so much that is evil has been done in the name of humanity's supposed gods that the first need is to do away with the religious motivation and argument altogether. Let us now, our doubter might say, by all means talk about how humanity should best conduct its affairs, but in a rational way, and with a proper regard for the reality of our situation.

We wish to argue, on the contrary, that God is essential if we are to take Jesus' teaching seriously. Creation can only have a purpose if it is designed and this requires a designer. And a designer, in turn, has some ideal design in view, in other words a purpose. If the evolutionary process were just a random kaleidoscope of chance events, why should we bother to care for our fellow human beings at all? The struggle each for our own success would be the only realistic principle to adopt, and even then we would have to acknowledge that we have no control over what actually happens. There would be, in this case, no ultimate goal toward which we are moving, nothing outside physical existence. Survival of the individual and, in the longer run, of the species would be the only criterion for success, and the only sense in which development could be said to occur is the emergence of species better fitted for survival. In this view, the more "developed" organisms are therefore just those with superior ability to survive.

But the situation is not as simple as this. Not all characteristics of organisms contribute simply to survival and we humans regard more than mere survival as of value. The first primitive organisms (bacteria and viruses) have survived without difficulty, more successfully than many more complex creatures that evolved later. Indeed, ultimately they may prove the most successful organisms of all by this criterion, for all we know of the future. There is absolutely no guarantee, therefore, in pure survival terms, that human beings represent a superior mutation. Who is to say that human behaviour may not eventually lead to the destruction of humanity? Hence we need to look further if we wish to find any deeper sense of purpose and evidence of development in the evolutionary process.

The current trend is to regard the standard of living or wealth as the main index of human "development". Modern "civilisation" attempts to reduce everything to this single index and to gear education, social pressures and human interchange to increasing wealth. A better standard of living will benefit survival of the individual and any dependants, so this overlaps in part with the criterion of survival. It can also enable a fuller and more rewarding life with more choice and reduced risks, though we have already seen that this is only true up to a certain point. Greater wealth does not guarantee greater happiness for an individual or nation, greater benefit to fellow human beings or greater affection.

Observation of human life, as we noted in the opening chapter, strongly suggests that we feel life has a purpose which amounts to something more than acquiring possessions, but often the search for this something more seems to degenerate into more elaborate answers to the same basic questions about what we can do to satisfy our bodily urges more fully. Tentative gropings emerge toward something described rather vaguely as "spiritual", but this may be no more than a search for unusual or aesthetic experiences or self-satisfaction. Nevertheless many doubt that the purpose of life is to satisfy our bodily urges primarily, with other people important only to the extent that they are useful or not in pursuit of that end.

It is not difficult to produce a list of factors which, in addition to satisfaction of our bodily needs, are generally agreed to contribute to a fulfilling life – freedom to choose our goals, to create in a variety of ways (from sublime works of art to beneficial inventions to simply growing fine plants), to experience excitement and beauty in a variety of ways, and to test and improve our abilities. Relations with others are of course crucial. We have noted that genes do not merely engage in a separate struggle for survival. They require co-operation in order to function satisfactorily. The whole body needs co-operation of all its parts for its well-being. Is this less true for the whole body of humankind? We want to be valued by others, to be able to do something "useful" in life. A sense of social isolation can double the chances of sickness or death (House *et al.*, 1988). Simply talking about troubles to another reduces the physiological effects of stress. And of course a close emotional relationship with another can be like heaven – or hell if it goes wrong! We need love, not necessarily sexual love, but acceptance and security from someone else. As children we flourished best in a secure and loving environment and as adults we certainly do not outgrow this childish need. But the world is all too often a harsh place and our needs may well remain inadequately fulfilled. We long for something more, greater love, greater understanding, greater ability to achieve something we cannot quite define. So we often grasp an assurance that there is another better state where all can be well, whether it is in a religious group of some sort on earth, or the promise of a wonderful life after death. Whatever it is we long for, mere survival of ourselves or of the human species is for most humans not the only or even the most important criterion for a fulfilling life. If all life depends merely on chance and conflict, such longings for something more are self-deceiving illusions, but if there is a God with a purpose for the creation, then they are, perhaps, part of that purpose.

But, as we have argued earlier, the basic flaw in this human longing throughout history has been its persisting concern with selfish ends, the desire for satisfaction and comfort each for our own needs, failing to grasp that only through a complete reversal of our current thinking can we begin to get anywhere near our dreams. This new way of thinking, as we keep stressing, was the primary concern of Jesus' teaching, based on his understanding of God's purpose. Hence the whole approach is underpinned by his belief in a creator God with a plan and a purpose.

The second reason why his teaching requires a God figure is that there is no hope of its implementation by human beings acting on their own, driven as they believe they are by the imperatives of the struggle for survival. Jesus promised a Guide and Supporter who would assist in implementing the necessary change in attitudes and motivations that he advocated, and we will come to this notion of the Holy Spirit below.

So Jesus bases everything on the existence of a god, for whom he claims to speak. But, and this is absolutely crucial, the God whom Jesus claimed to represent was pictured by him as totally different from other gods that human beings have devised throughout history to support their own inclinations. His God, he suggested, was not the dictatorial figure often depicted in the Old Testament with a special role for a particular group of people, and he, Jesus, had come to show what he is really like. Unfortunately Jesus' totally different portrayal of God is often obscured by the way in which Jesus has been interpreted by the Christian church subsequently. We now discuss these differences in detail and then we need to address questions of why we should put any reliance in what Jesus is reported to have said.

Why should we believe that he, rather than all the others who have made such claims, did actually have a private line to God? In any case, how do we know that what is recorded in the Bible has any basis of truth at all? It could be a total invention or a major distortion of what actually happened.

Jesus' view of God in contrast to traditional gods

Jesus suggested that the picture his hearers had of God was wrong on many counts, such as their belief that God has laid down rules to be followed in order to please him, that he punishes individuals directly for sinning in certain specific ways, that he insists on certain specific rites of worship and that he rules by exercising power. We develop these four themes in turn.

God has not laid down fixed rules

First Jesus claimed that God was not concerned with giving a set of rules and regulations. He was highly critical of those who had done just that, in the belief that they were reflecting the will of God. The dangers of self-righteousness and dismissal of others for their failures to live up to those standards were all too clear to him. He pointed them out pretty ruthlessly, simply because he could see all too vividly the harm they did to those who prided themselves on their own excellence and the resulting tendency for others to be rejected as failures and rejects in God's sight. "God is not like that and I have come to make that point pretty forcefully", he seems to have been saying. On the contrary, said Jesus, God loves his creation to a degree we cannot fathom and has a purpose for it, and his life and words demonstrate this. The ruling principle of the universe is one of "cosmic generosity" (Powell, 1998, p. 116), rather than restrained bullying. The world is not as God wants it to be, but there is a better way and Jesus has demonstrated it. To achieve this, humans must become like Jesus himself in their love for others, no longer driven by self-interest. Though this sounded impossible to those who heard him and, in the light of genetic theory as widely understood today, may sound even more impossible to our generation, Jesus claimed that it can happen because God's love can work within us, as it did in him. This is completely at odds with the standard religious injunction to achieve salvation by accepting unchanging "truths" and implementing unchanging rules (but otherwise carry on according to one's usual inclinations). Jesus suggests that we have to be open to being changed in unpredictable ways. And Jesus not only claimed to speak for God, but to demonstrate how humans could realise God's design.

Could God really be like this? Surely it would be uncomfortable. Jesus affirms that he is. Was it not intelligible that human beings, particularly religious leaders, would want to be rid of him, just because of what he was saying and above all what he was saying about God? Could one live with a God like that? Moreover, is it because he is like this that throughout history we human beings have found him unsatisfactory in so many ways and tried to mould him to suit ourselves? Yet haven't we now gone far enough along the road of trying to make him like ourselves? Do we not need to understand now what it might really mean for us to live in a true relationship with him as he is?

A typical example of how Jesus scandalised the "righteous" by demonstrating his refusal to accept the conventional view of God's rules occurs in Chapter 8 of the Fourth Gospel (John 8, 1–11). An incident is described which is of uncertain location in the text. In some texts it is absent and, where it is included, its position varies. It is as if the early Church was uneasy about it and may even have tried to remove it, but the story has survived nevertheless, even though it disturbs those who want a clear moral line. We see Jesus faced by the authorities with a test of his orthodoxy. They have found a woman caught in the act of adultery. What will this maverick do about it? Surely they have caught him this time. It is as if they have a good idea that he will avoid the "correct" response and give them another weapon to use against him. Jesus, however, adroitly turns the tables by suggesting that the one without sin can start the ritual stoning. In the face of this pointed suggestion and his subsequent apparent indifference they are nonplussed, showing that they had some residual shame that could be awakened by the challenge. Despite the fact that they previously claimed to keep the law, they felt unable to meet the challenge. Jesus refuses to condemn the woman, and tells her to go and sin no more. Thus he refuses to fixate on a particular act, but apparently makes a deeper point about her whole life and attitude. For Jesus it is not law, but attitude of mind in those seeking the punishment, that is important. For the woman he offers a command and the freedom to accept or reject it. We know no more.

John 8, 1–11

Jesus went to the Mount of Olives. Early on he was again in the temple and all the people came to him and he sat down and taught them. But the scribes and Pharisees brought a woman who had been caught in adultery and stood her in the middle and said to him, "Teacher, this woman was caught in the act of adultery. In the law, Moses commanded us to stone such women. What then do you say?" They said this to test him, so that they might have something to charge him with. But Jesus bent down and wrote with his finger on the ground. When they continued to ask him, he looked up and said to them, "Let the one of you that is sinless be the first to throw a stone at her." And he bent down again and wrote on the ground. And his listeners left one by one, beginning with the older ones. And Jesus was left on his own with the woman in the middle. Jesus looked up and said to her, "Woman, where are they? Has no-one condemned you?" She said, "No-one, Master." Jesus said, "Nor do I condemn you. Go and from now on don't sin any more."

This incident offers an archetypal example of human delight in catching out and condemning someone else for anything deemed particularly unacceptable, without regard to any lawlessness, lovelessness and persistent failure which may exist in one's own life. Such tendencies are particularly directed at the more vulnerable members of society (the poor, single mothers, asylum seekers, the homeless, the unemployed and so on). In the present case it is likely that they regarded a woman as an easy target and highly unlikely that they would ever have hauled a man up before him in this way. Some religiously based law even now is equally harsh, imposing the chopping off of hands for theft or death for sex before marriage or adultery (for women). In this incident Jesus refutes such hypocrisy and the punitive attitude associated with it. It may be argued that elsewhere he urges us to pluck out our eyes or cut off our hands when they offend us (Matthew 18, 8; Mark 9, 43), but this reads more like a vivid emphasis rather than a literal injunction, since clearly it is not the eye or hand which can be at fault, but the person, and the responsibility cannot be shifted.

The fundamental failures in life, he suggests, are not the petty "sins" of failing to obey some supposedly divine rules or even the misdemeanours which the "righteous" love to point to in others, but are typified in the failure of the so-called righteous even to consider that their own way is fundamentally flawed, that they are slaves to a meaningless system and that a richer and enriching freedom is on offer. Conventional views about goodness and badness need total rethinking. He asks for change, but a change that brings openness to new enlightenment rather than another set of rules and preoccupations.

God is not punitive

Second, Jesus denies that God is vengeful. The healing of the man born blind (John 9, 1–41) starts with Jesus' denial that some sin of the parents or the man is responsible. His God is not like that. It might be thought that such ideas have now been outgrown and there is now nothing radical about Jesus' denial of them. Nevertheless even an England football manager and a Vatican bishop (*The Guardian*, 5 February 2002) have declared such a viewpoint in recent times.

However, Jesus did on one occasion urge a man whom he had healed to sin no more, lest something worse befall him, namely the man healed at the pool of Bethesda (John 5, 1–18, see p.105), and this creates some difficulty for our interpretation of the present case. Jesus clearly refuted the prevailing notion that the only way of treating wrong-doers was to inflict some physical punishment on them, as we have seen in the story of the woman above. He also says we should forgive times without number (Matthew 18, 22) and he certainly does not present God as a severe judge. So why this exhortation in just this case of healing, but not in many others? Perhaps there was some specific feature of the particular case or the man that led him to use this method of urging him to use his newly achieved health for good rather than a personal pleasure spree. The injunction was not given immediately after he healed the man, but after the man had been quizzed by the Pharisees, so alternatively perhaps Jesus was warning him not to succumb to their attempts to persuade him to incriminate Jesus with false evidence.

Returning to the case of the man born blind, not for the first time Jesus heals on the Sabbath and is criticised for this. There is a discussion of the parallels between the physical blindness which he has cured and psychological or spiritual blindness which refuses to be cured. In the present case the latter takes the form of carping about when the deed was done and refusing to rejoice at the cure of a disability and the new life that was offered. His enemies claim the power to decide what is correct and what is not, and refuse to accept any deviation from this. Such situations are all too common, whatever the level of power involved, for power resists a challenge to its authority in every human context.

John 9, 1–41

As he was passing he saw a man who had been blind from birth. And the disciples asked him, "Rabbi, who did wrong, this man or his parents to make him be blind?" Jesus answered, "Neither he nor his parents did wrong, but it was to show God's deeds in him. We have to do the work of him who sent me while it is day. The night is coming when no-one can work. When I am in the world, I am the light of the world."

Having said this, he spat on the ground and made mud from the spittle and anointed the man's eyes with the mud. And he said to him, "Go and wash in the pool of Siloam" (this means "sent"). So he went away and washed and came back with his sight.

The neighbours and those who had seen him before as a beggar said, "Isn't this the one who sat and begged?" Some said that it was the man, others said it was not but they looked alike. He said, "I am the man." So they said to him, "How were your eyes opened?" He answered, "The man called Jesus made mud and anointed my eyes and said to me, 'Go to the pool of Siloam and wash' I went and washed, therefore, and I was able to see." And they said to him, "Where is this man?" He said, "I don't know."

They led the man who had been blind to the Pharisees. It was the Sabbath on the day when Jesus made mud and opened the man's eyes. The Pharisees asked him again, therefore, how he became able to see. He said to them, "He put mud on my eyes and I washed and I have my sight." So some of the Pharisees said, "This man is not from God, because he does not observe the Sabbath", but others said, "How can a wrong-doer achieve such signs?" And there was division among them. So they said to the man who had been blind, "You, what would you say about him, now that he has opened your eyes?" He said that this man was a prophet.

Jesus' God and His Purpose

So the Jewish leaders did not believe that the man had been blind and was able to see, until they had summoned his parents and asked them, "Is this your son, whom you say was born blind? How then can he now see?" His parents answered, "We know this is our son and he was born blind. How he can now see, we don't know, nor do we know who it was that opened his eyes. Ask him, he's old enough to speak for himself." His parents said this because they were afraid of the Jewish authorities, for the authorities had decided that, if anyone should accept that Jesus was the anointed one, he would be banished from the synagogue. For this reason the parents said that he was old enough to be questioned.

Therefore they called up the man who had been blind a second time and said to him, "Give the glory to God. We know that this man is a wrong-doer." So he replied, "I don't know if he is a wrong-doer. One thing I do know, that I was blind and now I can see." So they said to him, "What did he do to you? How did he open your eyes?" He replied, "I've told you already and you didn't hear. Why do you want to hear it again? You don't want to become his disciples too, do you?" And they poured contempt on him and said, "You are one of his disciples, but we are disciples of Moses. We know that God spoke to Moses, but we don't know where this man comes from." The man answered them, "Well, this is a surprise, that you don't know where he is from and he opened my eyes. We know that God doesn't listen to wrong-doers, but if anyone is God-fearing and does God's will, God listens to him. Since the beginning of time no-one has been known to open the eyes of a man born blind. If this man were not from God, he couldn't have done anything." They answered him, "You were born totally sinful, yet you are teaching us?" And they threw him out.

Jesus heard that they had thrown him out and found him and said, "Do you believe in the son of man?" He answered, "And who is he, Master, so that I may believe in him?" Jesus said to him, "You have seen him and the man who is talking to you, that's him." He said, "I believe, Master." And he bowed down before Jesus.

And Jesus said, "I came to sort out this world, so that those who cannot see would see and those who can see would become blind." Those from among the Pharisees who were with him heard this and said to him, "We aren't blind, are we?" But Jesus said to them, "If you were blind you would not be wrong-doers. But now you say that you can see, your wrong-doing persists."

God has not laid down fixed rituals of worship

Third, Jesus denies that God requires worship in a special authorised form. Before him the prophets had more than once contrasted the formalities of worship with true service of God. For example "I hate your religious festivals ... Instead let justice flow like a stream" (Amos, 5, 21ff.). Jesus makes the point many times. It is made forcibly in the later stages of his meeting with a Samaritan woman (John 4, 4–30). The account of this meeting also emphasises again the possibility of a new way of seeing things which Jesus can open up, and offers numerous other insights into his way of thinking. The details given suggest strongly that it was a real event, the memory of which has been preserved by Jesus telling it to one of his disciples or the woman recounting it to someone afterwards.

For a start, no Jew liked to speak to a Samaritan; even worse this was a woman and one who was coming on her own to the well at a time when the respectable women did not, so it was obvious to anyone of the time that she was a dubious character. A man who was willing to address her might also have been regarded as of dubious morality. So immediately we see Jesus refusing to accept the "us and them" divisions of the current religion-based morality. The disciples, as a result, cannot understand what he is up to and good Jewish tradition can hardly have concocted this episode. Jesus just ignores all the usual human barriers and can go straight from a normal request for a drink to expound the heart of his teaching.

John 4, 4–30

He had to go through Samaria, so he came to a city of the Samaritans called Sychar, near the piece of land that Jacob gave to his son Joseph. Jacob's spring was there. Therefore Jesus, being tired from his journey, sat down by the spring. It was about midday.

A Samaritan woman came to draw water. Jesus said to her, "Give me a drink", for his disciples had gone into the town to buy food. The Samaritan woman said to him, "How can you, a Jew, ask for a drink from me, a Samaritan woman?" For Jews and Samaritans don't mix together. Jesus answered her, "If you knew God's gift and who it is asking you for a drink, you would have asked him and he would have given you living water." She said to him, "Master, you don't have a bucket and the well is deep. Where do you get the living water? Surely you aren't greater than our father Jacob who gave us the well and drank from it himself, and his sons and his animals." Jesus answered her, "Everyone who drinks from this water will be thirsty again. Whoever drinks from the water which I give will not be thirsty for all eternity, but the water that I give will become a spring of water in him, springing up into eternal life." The woman said to him, "Master, give me this water, so that I won't be thirsty or come here to draw water." He said to her, "Go and call your husband and come here." She replied, "I don't have a husband." Jesus said to her, "You speak well in saying 'I don't have a husband.' You have had five husbands and the one you have now is not your husband. You spoke the truth." The woman said to him, "Master, I see you are a prophet. Our fathers worshipped on this mountain. And you people say that Jerusalem is the place where we ought to worship." Jesus said to her, "Believe me, woman, the hour is coming when you will worship the Father neither on this mountain nor in Jerusalem. [You worship what you don't know. We worship what we do know, because salvation is from the Jews.] But the hour is coming and is now here, when the genuine worshippers will worship the Father in spirit and in truth, for the Father does indeed look for such worshippers. God is spirit and those who worship him must worship him in spirit and in truth." The woman said to him, "I know that Messiah is coming, who is called the anointed one. When he comes, he will tell us everything." Jesus said to her, "I, who am talking to you, am he."

And at this, his disciples arrived and were amazed that he was talking with a woman. However, nobody said, "What are you looking for or why are you talking to her?" So the woman left her water jar and went into the town and said to the men, "Come and see a man who told me all I had done. Surely this is the anointed one." They went out of the town and came to him.

Apart from the rejection of tribal and sexual divisions, there are two key issues in this episode. Jesus provides "water" which will nurture the really significant living in this life which he refers to so often (see the discussion with Nicodemus earlier) and which is also the basis for eternal life, because living in and through him, inspired by his example, will not cease at this body's death but will find expression in a new dimension. Secondly, there is the whole issue of what worship really means. The word used refers originally to prostrating oneself before a god or secular lord as a sign of submission. However, it seems that there was more concern among religious authorities about where and when and how the outward trappings should be observed than the essential meaning. The Christian churches are not exempt, with special buildings (often reserved for a special performance for one hour a week and regarded by many worshippers as especially "sacred" and not to be desecrated by any other activities of the human beings that God created), robes of different colours for different seasons, special marks to separate those who may and may not carry out specific aspects of the rituals, special rules of procedure, involvement with all sorts of state pomp, especially pomp with military connotations, and so on. Jesus says that true worshippers will worship in spirit and in truth (and refers to God as "spirit"). He does not elaborate on this statement but the implications from the picture he paints of God would seem to be clear, that worship is more than a few religious exercises at set times. It must be a total way of life, not something done at a particular time and place. If it is not a total thing, it is nothing, because God is not central when other concerns intrude. This does not of course mean that some obsessive demonstration of forbidding godliness is required to pervade the whole of life, but rather that life should be lived in accordance with the creative love of God. Nor does it mean that no time should be set aside for special concentration on Jesus' words, under the Holy Spirit's guidance, only that this should be a means to something more, not an end in itself.

The woman is taken aback by his request for a drink, but not overawed, and asks him how he can make such a request from her. As often, Jesus immediately proceeds beyond the physical and introduces the notion that there is something on offer beyond the satisfaction of normal physical thirst. The woman is puzzled and probably sceptical – how will he provide water and how can the water he provides be any better than Jacob's legacy? Jesus says that what he has to offer will give her life of a completely different sort. She almost mocks him – that would be a great boon, as she would be free from coming to the well, at the hottest time of the day, what is more. Jesus picks up the point and asks to see her husband, and when she demurs he displays a detailed insight into her history. This impresses the woman deeply, and she moves on to one of the major disputes between the Samaritans and the Jews, whether or not Jerusalem was the proper place to worship God or whether the Samaritans' alternative mountain site was adequate for the purpose. Jesus states clearly that such divisions are meaningless and that soon the real nature of such worship will be known. God does not require a special place of worship but needs to be worshipped "in spirit and in truth". (The assertion that the Samaritans don't know what they are talking about, while the Jews do, seems intrusive and does not tally well with Jesus' usual attitude or the general picture of "the Jews" in this Gospel, who are shown as the enemies of the truth that Jesus stood for, so it may be an editorial insertion from a later date.) The woman is aware of the promise of a Messiah who will clarify all the present disputes and uncertainty. Jesus simply states that he is that person. She is so impressed that she goes and talks to the men of the village, who are probably more willing to listen to her than the women would be! Jesus further demonstrated his refusal to accept human barriers and divisions by staying for two days in the Samaritan town, we are not told in whose house!

This difference in the nature of the God whom Jesus portrayed has radical implications for the way in which we should think about prayer. Prayers become too often lists of requests to God to do this and that which we think would be a good idea if God would just turn his mind in that direction. The practice of confession assumes that we know what is wrong with us, which is too often quite untrue. Even if we assume that God is busying himself with every detail of the world's and our own affairs, surely we must believe that he has his own agenda, which he is hardly likely to revise if a few people ask him to change it, especially when, as so often, some others are asking for the exact opposite. The Lord's Prayer includes the phrase "Thy will be done", but it is somewhat doubtful if that is really what most of us want, even though too often we say it as a sort of unloading of responsibility, leaving the problems for God to sort out while we go our own way regardless, or resignedly if things are not going our way.

True prayer is listening, changing and acting, rather than simply asking, and so doing God's will rather than asking him to do ours. If God is the recipient of endless prayers to do something about the poor of the world, the sick of the world, could he not arguably be wearied, not by the poor and sick of whom he is deeply aware if Jesus is anything to go by, but by the source of these prayers, primarily the affluent in western society at least, who refuse to do much that lies within their own powers about the poor and the sick of the world? This is but one of the many contradictions which characterise the present state of affairs. There is no reason to suppose that God will miraculously cure the ills of the poor or oppressed or afflicted without some change in the state of the rich and influential and flourishing, whether this is to be voluntary or involuntary. But of course the rich and influential and flourishing don't want to admit that.

Jesus indicated that prayers should be private and brief and gave the Lord's Prayer as a pattern to his disciples. This focuses far more on acknowledging the nature of God than making a series of requests. So for a statement of his priorities we can scarcely do better than turn to this prayer which is still used by all Christians today. It is familiar and familiarity blunts the impact, but it repays much careful consideration (Matthew 6, 7–13). Again we use Matthew's version rather than Luke's shorter version.

Matthew 6, 7–13

Our Father in heaven,
Thy name be hallowed.
Thy kingdom come,
Thy will be done, as in Heaven, so on earth.
Give us our daily portion of bread today.
And forgive us our debts, as we have forgiven our debtors.
And do not bring us to a time of testing,
But save us from evil.

"Our Father in heaven."

Jesus persistently referred to God as his father ("Daddy" is the nearest word to the one he used), not an awesome distant forbidding being, but as close as a human relationship can be (while admitting that most fathers are not ideal and some are very far from it; perhaps "mother" might in some respects have been a better term, but not for his audience at the time). Nevertheless this Father does exist in a different way from us. And he knows each of us like a father knows his children, our weaknesses and strengths, our fears and hopes. He does not condemn us, but supports us and teaches and guides us. Though Luke's version does not have "Our", Matthew does, emphasising that we do not pray as isolated individuals, but share together.

"Thy name be hallowed."

"The name" signified, as in the case of the name of Jesus, all that is consistent with God as he is and has shown himself in Jesus to be. This is a positive affirmation that God should be revered and regarded as occupying an essential place in our own thinking. It is a statement of faith and of what our priorities are or should be.

"Thy kingdom come."

We often rattle this off without real commitment to doing anything about it. So much of western "civilisation", which claims to be Christian, indicates this, as illustrated in detail in earlier chapters. This kingdom demands mighty changes in priorities to match up to the way of living outlined by Jesus as God's purpose, and the prayer commits us to these changes.

"Thy will be done: as in Heaven, so on earth."

The message is not about some better life beyond the grave, but about living by the priorities of God here. This ends the first section of the prayer which commits us to God's priorities. For many that suggests a cramping of style, rather than a fuller life as Jesus stresses. We have tried to show that this is a major misconception. (Luke does not have this phrase.)

"Give us our daily portion of bread today."

The word usually translated as "daily" bread only occurs here in the New Testament, so the meaning is a little uncertain, but this is the most likely interpretation. The "us" includes everyone. A modest petition, not for all the things we might, as human beings, want for ourselves, nor a series of requests on behalf of others. God knows their needs and ours, we don't have to recite a lot of petitions, which usually go no further. If we do pray for others, it should be to let God remind us of what we might be doing for them. So all we have here is a reminder that the basics will be enough. Though prosperity has been so often seen as a mark of God's approval, this is very different.

"And forgive us our debts, as we have forgiven our debtors."

A hard one. If we can't forgive, there's not much hope in prospect for us. Just claiming the Christian label is not adequate. There's no favoured treatment for the Christian, nor are we expected to treat the non-Christian differently. We cannot understand God's forgiveness unless we can experience our own, just as we cannot understand his love unless we can give love ourselves. If our minds are set in a mould of refusal to forgive, they are closed to different messages and influences, and cannot accept properly the offer of God's forgiveness. Giving is necessary in order to understand receiving. Many of those bereaved by the September 11th atrocity urged forgiveness rather than revenge, but the majority of a supposedly Christian nation clamoured for revenge and the authorities chose this path. (Luke, rather unrealistically, asserts that we do forgive all those who are indebted to us!)

"And do not bring us to a time of testing" (or "lead us not into temptation" in the familiar form, or "ordeal" is another possible meaning).

A bit problematical, especially as Jesus himself was tested, and many of his followers too. We have been arguing that God wants humans to grow and develop beyond their present childish state of wanting more than others, and hence we will be tested, just as children need to be, so that we can learn a better way. Jesus surely realised this. Hence this request seems odd. It is almost as if we have reverted to a picture of a god who tries out his followers to see who will produce what he wants, and the petition is asking to be rescued from this test. One is tempted to suggest, though without any support from variations in the text, that it would make more sense if it read, "And when you bring us to the time of testing, save us from evil."

"But save us from evil."

Jesus would have realised how easily temptation can be succumbed to, often not so much through straightforward desire to do the wrong thing, but through self-deceit about what is right and what is not, and the ambiguities present in all human situations. Here the need for clarity of thought (pureness of heart), regard for the truth, humility and so forth is fundamental.

The common addition to the prayer, "For thine is the kingdom, the power and the glory" only appears in some of the ancient texts and may be a later addition.

God does not exercise power in the way that humans do

Fourth, Jesus denies that God works in the world by exercising power in the way that secular leaders exercise it. We have already discussed in the last chapter Jesus' refusal to play the power game, as shown in the allegorical story of the Temptations and in the account of the Last Supper in the Fourth Gospel, and this point does not need any further elaboration.

Other gods

But what of the gods that humanity has gravitated towards through many centuries? These gods who crowd through human history are very different from the God whom Jesus portrays. Human observation of nature shows that there must be forces at work beyond our comprehension. Let us see, the thinking goes, if we can establish contact with them and influence them. Hence the concept of hidden forces in nature develops and ways of influencing these forces are tried out. The forces are given individual existence as supernatural beings and, not surprisingly, it is assumed that the psychology of these beings is very similar to human psychology and they need persuading by the same means as humans use to influence each other. These forces are believed to be present in particular places and their presence must be respected. They are local and restricted in their influence. A bargain is devised, whereby these forces offer protection (somewhat intermittently) if they are given appropriate gifts. Sometimes the gifts don't work and an explanation is easily found in some failure to carry out the ritual correctly or the failings of some unfortunate individual. However, it is believed that the forces, if treated properly, will favour the group that makes the bargain against other groups who do not recognise them. Our group thus has special qualities that separate it from all others, who lack these favoured attributes. (The problem, though, is that other groups also have their own favoured attributes and look down on those who do not have them.) The supposed nature of these forces or beings is based on existing human nature, with all its motives and limitations, and such ideas are resistant to change. The question of whose gods are stronger is settled by very human means.

These attempts at explaining how the world works in due course develop into more sophisticated religious forms, embracing a wider range of events and envisaging a wider scope for the god, often under the influence of some individual making special claims to religious insight, but the original ideas are still apparent even in the "higher" religions which survive today. Attributions of human-like characteristics to the god based on human requirements are refined and extended, but the human basis is still present. For example, for the majority of followers the god is seen as existing at a particular place (the mosque, synagogue, church or shrine) and on a larger scale in particular cities such as Jerusalem, Mecca or Rome. For many this includes the Christian God who lives in "the house of God" (or rather "houses"!), a place which must be treated with special reverence, despite the "official" view that God is everywhere. And the human face of the god is particularly evident in arbitrary rules supposedly handed down from on high, but principally designed to demonstrate the uniqueness of the followers. So religions tend to lay stress on externals like what is worn or not worn, eaten or not eaten, what parts of the body should be washed or shaved or visible and when and where, even if this is reduced to a token act. They lay stress on preserving traditions laid down in a sacred text, they insist on specialist intermediaries between the faithful and the god. Above all, through these characteristics they have a potential for division and strife with those who are different.

Religions have typically been used to reinforce or create political divisions, serving the existing earthly powers. And religions typically have a persistent anti-feminine streak, suppressing the rights of women and often physically abusing them for imaginary sins, such as witchcraft, and sexual "misdemeanours" which are tolerated in men.

Many attribute the evils wrought by religions as due to the perverse influence of faith, which they compare with reason, depicting faith as "blind trust, in the absence of evidence, even in the teeth of the evidence" (e.g. Dawkins, 1989, p. 198). Crimes of persecution and violence against others are not, however, unequivocally due to the influence of faith, as some would claim. Religions have been guilty of many crimes against humanity, but secular systems supposedly based on reason have not been markedly exempt from similar acts, as seen in the recent history of communism. Furthermore, faith is not restricted to religions. Every action we take requires faith that our presuppositions, which enable us to predict the consequences, still hold. We could not check every presupposition before every action or we would remain immobile, so we have to proceed with faith.

The failure of such "faith" is devastating to life and personality, producing irrational anxieties of many different types and in its worst form, psychosis. Moreover, the so-called rationalists depend on assumptions they have made about the nature of logic, reliability of their observations, functioning of their own central nervous systems and so forth. Every scientist has to make assumptions (a less emotive word for faith) in order to proceed with experimental studies, or perpetual doubt would prevent any steps to better knowledge. The final choice is not therefore between faith and reason, but depends on which set of assumptions we choose as the most likely to provide a sound basis for proceeding.

In religions it is where faith is directed and the nature of the supposed object of faith that presents the problem. In the main, faith has been directed toward some object that is nothing more than a human creation with no reliable basis outside human nature. It then bears all the signs of its origins and produces the consequences we often see. But equally a faith in a master race or "the people" can produce horrors equal to any that religions focussed on a god can claim. The problem lies in the human motivations in both cases.

Religions may also claim to put their adherents in contact with the god and to offer a special "spiritual" experience, and therefore another aspect of "more spontaneous" religious practices is often the claim to direct communion with the god in some form of ecstatic or trance-like display, or "speaking with tongues", which in its less extreme manifestations may simply take the form of expressions of extreme happiness in worship of the deity. This too, however, can often become a ritualised display of loyalty and gratitude for the gifts the deity has distributed in the past and a hope that these will continue. Such religion does not solve the real problems of humanity, but merely makes it easier to ignore the big issues by providing a safe cocoon to withdraw into and make the believer feel at ease.

Thus the central claim of religions and their founders, either overtly or covertly, is that in some way contact has been established with the god and a set of commands has been conveyed from the god to humans telling them how to achieve favour and continued contact with the god, and promising that if these commands are followed, the god will look favourably on the followers. Religions offer the illusion of secure certainty, often producing self-satisfaction, intolerance and inflexibility. Originally the promised favours took the form of material comforts, but attempts to deal with the problem that these did not always arrive led to the notion that the rewards would come in a future life. After all, if the gods' existence is in some way different from our earthly physical existence, maybe we too can enter into that other existence. And this other existence will surely be superior to the earthly one – Heaven for the Christian, Paradise for the Muslim, for the Buddhist escape to Nirvana from a world "split into disjointed parts" where "no-one really belongs to anyone else" (Conze, 1959, p. 110). The implication of such religious beliefs for life here is only that certain commands must be followed in order to escape from that life, such as those described earlier (regular praying, dietary and dress laws, symbolic cleansing) and perhaps some rules about relations with others. But basically the message is always about the way to "save" oneself.

The Jewish Torah elaborated the original commandments into a multiplicity of precise rules on how life was to be lived by the chosen people, in order that they might continue to enjoy the favour of Jahweh. The Koran begins each section with the assertion that Allah is compassionate and merciful, but otherwise is full of threats about the punishment awaiting the non-believer and the reward of Paradise for faith and good works (e.g. Dawood, 1999, pp. 47, 73 and passim). Fear of God is the key to prosperity (ibid., p. 53). Doing more than the minimum will produce greater rewards. The "additional duty" of praying at night (in addition to the required times of day) will lead to being exalted "to an honourable station" (ibid., p. 203). "Deeds of lasting merit shall earn you a better recompense in the sight of your Lord and a more auspicious end" (ibid., p. 219). "For the unbelievers We have prepared chains and fetters and a blazing fire" (ibid., p. 413). The same message resonates again and again throughout the text -- do what I demand or it will be the worse for you! Ultimately it is what you believe that counts in your favour, not how you behave.

The Buddhist scriptures (Conze, 1959) are not, of course, focussed on a single God, but claim to provide insight into the way the whole creation functions and how the individual can achieve the ultimate state of non-being through the appropriate exercises. There are 250 rules for monks to follow (ibid., p. 69). Rules of sexual morality are laid down for men (but not, it seems, for women!) (ibid., p. 71) and a vast list of offences to be avoided is specified (ibid., pp. 73 ff.). Evil deeds will inevitably lead to suffering (p. 83) and "If you want honour, wealth, or, after death, a blissful life among the gods, then take good care that you observe the precepts of a moral life" (ibid., p. 84). And trance is required to "win the dharmas which finally allow us to gain that highest state, so hard to reach, which is tranquil, ageless and deathless" (ibid. p., 47). Other human beings are of no importance – "a person is not more firmly associated with his own people than birds who flock together ... no-one really belongs to anyone else" (ibid., p. 110).

In more contemporary, less overtly religious manifestations, the promise of a better life after death has become less convincing in our supposedly rational age, so the message has often become directed toward achieving a "full" life here and now by employing some procedure which has become known in some magical way to a favoured individual (the Glastonbury bookshop phenomenon). More specific ways of achieving new dimensions of experience are promised through drugs or special exercises. As we have argued, religions, though they bind together their adherents, are first and foremost individualistic, focussing on exhorting the individual to take steps toward a better state hereafter, and the modern substitutes for religion follow a similar path though focussing on this life rather than the life hereafter. Though he made no such statements, Jesus' message has also been predominantly interpreted within the same mould of how to achieve salvation for oneself – be baptised, make your confession, carry out the prescribed penance, take communion, say your prayers and God will see you are all right. Ironically this happens even though an elaborate theoretical structure was established on the basis of Jesus' death and resurrection, which specifically stated that no such observations of rules and "sacrifices" was necessary and that faith alone would guarantee salvation.

Oddly, this theory was itself based on a ritual of sacrifice to satisfy God's righteousness. The early church struggled to work out the implications of Jesus' death and the nature and consequences of his resurrection. Why should such a good man suffer in this way? Indeed, if he really came from God (or even was God) could this make any sense at all? What could it possibly achieve? Through St Paul a solution came with the doctrine of the Atonement. Humanity, it was argued, had a debt to God in the form of sin, that is failure to match up to God's hopes for his creation. Such a debt should normally be paid off by punishment or sacrifice to keep God happy. But the debt is too big for this, because human sin is all-pervasive, so to give humanity a fresh start, God's son took all the punishment on himself by sacrificing his life. In essence this has the form of a primitive tale of sacrifice to mitigate the god's anger. It has little relation to anything that Jesus said. There is a single sentence, identical in both Mark's and Matthew's gospels (Mark 10, 5; Matthew 20, 28) where Jesus says he has come to give up his life "in redemption" for many. The word used refers to the price paid to free a slave and it occurs nowhere else in the New Testament. Hardly a firm foundation for a whole theology! It could refer to freeing humanity in all sorts of senses, and there is no good reason for adopting the special interpretation devised by Paul and subsequently adopted by the Church.

It might, however, be argued in a more straightforward way that Jesus' death demonstrated starkly and brilliantly exactly what he had been preaching, that the key struggle was between love, which creates and enriches life, and selfish competition (for power in this case) which divides and destroys. It was not, as religions typically proclaim, between one interpretation of supposed divine laws and another. One driving force in human society, the urge to control power, to define the in-group and suppress dissent, would be bound to react in exactly the way it did to the proposal for radical change. This was not a reaction unique to the Jewish authorities and due to their specific religious beliefs. Would not any human society treat God like this when it was clear that his nature was not as they had always assumed it to be and matching their requirements? The crucifixion crystallises humanity's total misunderstanding of what God is really like. We suggest that such an interpretation makes much better sense than the sacrificial explanation of Jesus' death, and we do not believe that these events needed the mystic interpretation which was built upon them, that Jesus chose to die in order to expiate the sins of humans.

The theory of sin and sacrifice linked Christianity to Old Testament Judaism (and many other religions) and was driven by Paul's wish to interpret Christ to the Jewish nation and his fixation with Jesus' death and resurrection, to the neglect of much of the teaching and healing acts which had characterised Jesus' life. It carried over the notion of the chosen people to the Christian

Church, with the consequences outlined above of a religious belief in a special status. Paul linked the notion of redemption to the Jewish myth of the Fall told in Genesis when Adam disobeyed God, developing the notion that God's original plan went awry because humans rebelled and God had to do something to put it all right again. Jesus supposedly, by his death in some mystical way, cancelled Adam's disobedience. But the story of the serpent and the apple (the Fall) told in Genesis, the first book of the Bible, is most plausibly interpreted as an attempt to explain humans' special ability to be aware of their actions and their power for good or ill, which represents the beginning of human consciousness and freedom of choice. We have been drawing out the central theme of Jesus' teaching, that he is offering the way to developing this freedom to a much higher level. This indicates that his goal is not so much to reverse the supposed effect of the Fall, restoring humanity to a pre-human state of innocence and ignorance, but rather to complete the process of increasing freedom and understanding. Jesus is concerned with human development, not another variation on the old religious theme of rules and rituals.

The original emphasis on faith alone was transmuted into the more mechanical routine of baptism, confession, absolution, Eucharist and so forth. The Reformation rebelled against this mechanistic view of salvation and re-emphasised the importance of faith. But even those branches of Christianity which are most hostile to the formalities of the older traditions have substituted their own alternative demands, requiring that the believer shall have experienced an authentic "born again" experience. To the impartial bystander it will seem that often not a lot else follows so far as life on this earth goes. Christians are often seen as people who claim to be good but fail to live up to this. The born-again Christian often seems to be even more free than the neighbouring agnostic to feel self-satisfied, to denigrate those of a different outlook, concentrate on achieving a comfortable life without too much regard for the consequences, particularly for those not too close to home, while observing some suitable marks of commitment such as attending services and doing a few acceptable good works.

God's Unfinished Business

In these ways and through many other ancient traditions, the aspiration for a god to give support and blessing here on earth, or here and hereafter, and in general to help in confronting the business of living in the physical world, with its constraints and suffering as well as its opportunities, has found outlets. The thrust has been substantially, "What will God do for me?" This has been modified to some extent by the thought of what God will do for the whole body of believers who are deemed to be part of some greater whole. This has of course meant only a limited awareness of "the other". Splits within religions have further restricted the range of loyalty. Hence religions meet certain human needs for support but comprehensively fail to heal the overriding needs of an angry and fragmented world. We have argued that Jesus' teaching, on the contrary, can do just that. But why should we believe his own claims about himself and God? We turn to this question in the next chapter.

Chapter 5
The Authority of Jesus

Why believe that Jesus spoke for God? On what grounds can it be argued that Jesus' claim to be speaking for God is any more acceptable than the claim of many others to be God-inspired? And why should anyone trust the records of what he said and did?

The Fourth Gospel (from which most of the quotations we have used have been drawn) is the only Gospel specifically claiming to include an eye-witness account of Jesus' life and teaching. We cannot emphasise too strongly that the focus must be on Jesus himself, if we are to understand anything of what is critical to the future of human kind. We would stress that, in our view, it is not the church or some reinterpretation of the gospels, but Jesus himself, what he said, what he did, that will give the key. But, of course, it is hard and at times seemingly impossible to know what in our records is a true record of Jesus himself. Much has been reinterpreted in the light of the understanding of the early Church, and of the apostle Paul in particular. Which means that we should focus on the gospels, and in particular on the one Gospel which claims and suggests a direct link back to someone who knew Jesus personally. In particular there are passages in that Gospel which have the "feel" of personal recollections of events passed on to the writer and marked by touches and details which indicate an individual recollection. For example, the account of Jesus' arrest and trial and crucifixion contains many details not given in any of the other gospels, strengthening the impression that it is based on direct experience. Here Peter is named as cutting off the ear of the High Priest's servant, named as Malchus. The disciple with Peter later that evening, was, we are told, well known to the

High Priest and was able to gain entry to the courtyard where the trial was held and to get Peter admitted as well. The details of the trial must have come from one of them, most probably this other disciple, as he remains an anonymous figure like the editor of the Gospel. (He may or may not be the same person as that other anonymous figure referred to as the beloved disciple.) It is possible, therefore, that this other disciple is a primary source of this Fourth Gospel. One suggestion has been that the source of this account and some of the other stories may have been Jesus' close friend, Lazarus, or someone from his circle. We know that Jesus talked a lot to Mary, the sister of Lazarus, so it is likely that he also had many discussions with his dear friend Lazarus. Subsequently one or more editors must have arranged the material, which could have been in an oral or a written form. There is, therefore, no firm argument against parts of the record dating from quite soon after the actual events.

Whatever the original source, we need to be fully aware that the complete Gospel was not committed to writing until some time later than the events. The Church believed that the second coming was imminent, so why bother to create perishable records? Hence what we have is the result of an edited version of the oral memories, sometimes with additions reflecting later thinking (such as constant references to "the Jews" as the source of all opposition to Jesus yet simultaneously as the source of all knowledge about God!). We need to bear in mind always the overall picture of Jesus' thinking and not take every statement as accurate, especially when it fits poorly into the general picture and fits neatly into the subsequent re-interpretation of the events.

It is often argued that the first three (Synoptic) gospels give a very different picture of Jesus from that presented in the Fourth Gospel. Though there are many differences in detail, the broad picture of what Jesus was trying to convey is consistent. The Synoptic Gospels do tend to concentrate on what the message was and show editorial differences in presentation of the material, while the Fourth Gospel is particularly concerned with pressing home Jesus' authority to say it, the links between God and Jesus and the authority and role of the Holy Spirit (the Adviser).

The Authority of Jesus

There have been many interpretations of the "real" message and intentions of Jesus in recent years and no attempt will be made here to survey and evaluate them. Many of these attempt to interpret Jesus as simply a man of his time, with human aspirations, purging from the record any elements that are not explicable in terms of the rational science and experience of a later time. On this view, his claim to speak with insight drawn from another sphere of being, his miracles, his raising of the dead to life and his own resurrection are all accretions designed to prove the early Church's case, and not reliable reports of what really happened. In fact, however, the accounts of the most dramatic elements in the story are amazingly matter-of-fact and "flat". They simply do not read like the ramblings of the confused, the fabrications of a sensation seeker or a concocted story designed to dazzle the credulous. For example, when Jesus appears to his disciples after his resurrection, there are none of the trappings of divine sensationalism and they are not able to recognise him at first. Instead, he simply greets them with the normal salutation or invites them to take some food. Unless these accounts are an extraordinarily subtle double bluff, and more sophisticated than we could imagine, one is tempted to believe that they are indeed the most straightforward accounts those present could offer of the experiences they had. And attempts to explain away the Resurrection and the post-Resurrection appearances remain on the whole tortuous and unsuccessful (see Frank Morison's book, *Who Moved the Stone?* (1958), an appraisal by an initially sceptical lawyer of the evidence for the Resurrection, which concludes that it cannot readily be explained away in more "normal" ways).

To take an example of one attempt to interpret Jesus in purely human terms, he has been pictured as a failed political revolutionary, who hoped to re-establish the kingdom of Israel on earth, and after his failure to achieve this, his life and teaching were reinterpreted in terms of another extra-terrestrial kingdom. This is highly unconvincing. Not only is there no indication in the New Testament to support such a view, but he is specifically shown as refusing to respond to temptation from the Devil (Matthew 4,1–11; Mark 1, 12–13; Luke 4, 1–13) or the people (John 6, 15) to become a king and he demonstrates his "power" by washing the disciples' feet (John 13, 1–17)! Moreover, another independent source, the Jewish historian Josephus, gives not the slightest sign that Jesus was a revolutionary. Josephus (Antiquities 18, 33) says,

> At this time appeared Jesus, a wise man. For he was a doer of startling deeds, a teacher of people who receive the truth with pleasure. And he gained a following both among Jews and among many of Greek origin. And when Pilate, because of an accusation made by the leading men among us, condemned him to the cross, those who loved him previously did not cease to do so. And up until this very day the tribe of Christians (named after him) has not died out.

Why, if Jesus was just another in the long line of failed Jewish revolutionaries against the occupying power, should his teaching and influence have survived even for a few months, let alone until the time when the gospels were written many years later? Furthermore, not only the supernatural elements in the record would have to be explained as added after the event, but in fact the majority of the record fails to fit this interpretation. Such injunctions as "Pay to Caesar what belongs to Caesar" (Matthew 22, 21), "love your enemies" (Matthew 5, 43), "my kingdom is not of this world" (John 18, 36), "you must be born from above" (John 3, 7), "Do not be anxious about tomorrow" (Matthew 6, 34) and his attitudes to such matters as money, women and children are all completely alien to the role suggested. They would simply not have worked in the society of the day (and would not work in our own as currently organised, though we suggest that it is high time to try them out). So where did they come from, if not from Jesus himself? And in that case, he cannot have been talking about a kingdom in the usual sense of that word, with the world being run and power being exercised as it is at present, so he was either deranged (the preferred explanation of his enemies) or speaking a truth which is worth further investigation.

It is debatable exactly what Jesus meant by saying his kingdom was not "of this world". The words are usually interpreted as meaning that the kingdom will be in another (heavenly) place. However, the Greek words say literally "is not from this world" using the same word as in "a woman from Samaria" or "some people from John's disciples". And the original meaning of the word for world (cosmos) is "order". So the words could have meant that the new order cannot develop from the way things are at present. He adds that if his kingdom were of this world his followers would fight for him, but his kingdom cannot come out of that sort of action.

Clearly, whatever it was exactly that Jesus taught and did both astonished those who were sympathetic and horrified the authorities of the day. He was sufficiently at odds with their attitudes to cause a threat. If he was not preaching revolution, why was this? Even his enemies seem to have acknowledged the miracles, as in the case of the man born blind (John 9, 1–41/see p.80). Faced with this miracle, they made strenuous efforts to discredit it without success. If our record is just a fabrication, it is difficult to understand the hostility. Why did Jesus present such a threat? It could not have been simply that he claimed to be God's messenger. Many a prophet before him had made such a claim and, despite the biblical picture of persecuted prophets, they were usually listened to and even provoked change (after all in many cases their teaching survived in the written records). Rather it seems to have been the nature of the very different God he claimed to speak for that was offensive, a threat to the god of bargains whom the authorities represented and expounded and whose intermediaries they claimed to be, and to the requirements of public ritual and performance which they controlled, and which were the source of their power and wealth.

Ultimately there is no cast-iron proof that the picture we have of Jesus is invariably true to what he said and did or that his claims were true, but a consistent picture does emerge of the main aspects of his teaching. For some people none of this measures up to the standards required for the evidence to be trusted. But, as we have pointed out above, even the hard-nosed scientist takes a huge amount on trust. When he or she devises a new hypothesis to explain the facts available, this guides future investigation. The hypothesis may be a leap in the dark; it certainly is not established truth, but a basis for proceeding. In the same way, one can test the hypothesis that Jesus' teaching about the way life should be lived is valid and proceed to test whether it works by taking his offer seriously and living life accordingly. There is much that happens in the world that we cannot explain in terms currently available and a growing realisation that "alternatives" of all sorts are possible. There is a willingness to consider the possibility of radical change from accepted practice and to accept that final certainty, comforting though it might be, is bound to prove elusive. Jesus asks for trust and openness to change, with the promise that such openness will produce immense development in the human mind and human society.

Jesus' claims about himself

We will now look at a few passages from the Fourth Gospel to illustrate Jesus' claims about himself. First we consider Jesus' claim to speak with the authority of God and the implications of such a claim. He makes this claim frequently and explicitly, often embodying it in a reference to God as his father. Such a claim caused public offence to the authorities in part because of what it implied about their own authority.

An early example of such a claim in the Fourth Gospel occurs when Jesus heals a man at the pool of Bethesda (the traditional name, though in most cases the text says Bethzatha) (John 5, 1–18). Incidentally this account is of considerable interest because it provides a small indication that the record is reliable. The text says, "there is a pool by the Sheep Gate ... which has five porticoes". For years this was regarded as a mistake, since five porches would be an architectural oddity, but in the 1950s archaeologists found the double pool with two porches on each side and another in between them, confirming the account we have and reinforcing the belief that other details in this and other episodes in the Fourth Gospel are authentic (Fox, 1991, p. 246). Apart from this, the main significance of the episode is that it provokes a dispute with the authorities because Jesus healed on the Sabbath, demonstrating his disregard for the rigid observance of laws simply for their own sake. And he refers to God as his father, claiming a special relationship, even hinting rather mischievously that God is not averse to working on the Sabbath. This is the first time where such a reference is reported to cause public offence to the authorities. The implications of the claim are far reaching. If his claim is accepted and we want to know God, there is no more reliable source. He is either correct in his claim or a flagrant liar or unbalanced. If he is correct, other prevailing ideas about God need to be reconsidered, since in that case they would seem to be only the constructs of human minds. And what of the picture he paints of God which we have outlined above? Which sounds more plausible, that the God who created the world requires arbitrary rules to be observed by those who worship him, even if these perpetuate suffering, or that he wants the life he has given them to be full, creative and joyous, which is all wholly consistent with true worship of him?

John 5, 1–18

In Jerusalem there is a pool by the Sheep Gate called in Hebrew Bethzatha, which has five porticoes. In these porticoes there used to lie a host of sick people, blind, lame and paralysed. There was a man there who had been ill for 38 years. When Jesus saw this man lying there and knew he had been there a long time, he said to him, "Do you want to be healthy?" The sick man replied "Master, I don't have anyone to put me in the pool when the water is disturbed. While I am getting there, someone else climbs down in front of me."

Jesus said to him, "Get up, pick up your mat and walk about." And immediately the man became well and picked up his mat and walked about.

That day was the Sabbath, so the Jewish leaders said to the man who been cured, "It's the Sabbath and you are not supposed to be carrying your mat." But he answered, "The man who made me well said to me, 'Pick up your mat and walk about.'" They asked him, "Who is the man who said to you, 'Pick it up and walk about'?" But the man who had been cured didn't know who it was, for there was a crowd in the area and Jesus had gone away.

Afterwards Jesus found him in the temple and said to him, "Look, you have become well, don't do any more wrong lest something worse happen to you." The man went off and announced to the Jewish leaders that Jesus was the one who made him well. And after this the Jewish leaders went after Jesus because he was doing this on the Sabbath.

But Jesus answered them, "My father is at work right up until this moment and I too am at work." On this account, therefore, the Jewish leaders sought still more to kill him, not only because he was free with the Sabbath, but he also spoke of God as his own father, making himself equal to God.

In Chapter 7 of the Fourth Gospel (John 7, 10–24) Jesus appears in Jerusalem at the Festival of Tabernacles and teaches so impressively that the Jewish authorities wonder how an untrained man can display such wisdom. Jesus again claims that he has been sent by God and that this is the origin of his knowledge and that anyone who has any desire to follow God will be able to recognise whether his words match up to what God would want or are simply ideas of his own. He is not claiming any glory for himself, so what could be his motive other than to speak for God? If the Jewish authorities claim to speak for God but don't recognise Christ and if they claim to follow the Law but fail, that shows them up for what they are. Even they will break the Sabbath if the due day for circumcision happens to fall on it. They should stop judging by external criteria like whether the Sabbath is being observed and consider the more fundamental issues, for example that a man in need was healed. Thus Jesus is urging the need for unprejudiced perception of the true nature of what had been happening. Truth is not dependent on something laid down as inviolable in tradition. Understanding of truth requires openness to new insights and criteria. An unprejudiced judgement of his authenticity cannot easily dismiss his claims. Refusal to admit the truth due to self-interested bias is all too common and we have already given some examples of how the powers-that-be can manipulate "the truth" in their own interest.

John 7, 10–24

But when his brothers had gone up to the festival, then he went as well, not openly but secretly. The Jewish authorities, however, looked for him at the festival and said, "Where is that fellow?" And there was a great deal of debate about him among the people. Some said he was a good man, and others said, "No, on the contrary he is misleading the people." However no-one spoke out openly about him, because of their fear of the Jewish authorities.

Then, however, in the middle of the festival Jesus stood up in the temple and started teaching. At this the Jewish authorities were amazed and said, "How does this man, with no formal education, know our learned writers?" Jesus answered them, saying, "My teaching is not my own but comes from the one who sent me. If anyone wants to do his will, he will understand whether this teaching comes from God or whether I am speaking out on my own account. Anyone who speaks out on his own account is seeking his private glory, but if anyone seeks the glory of the one who sent him, he is truthful and there's no wrong in him. Didn't Moses give you the Law? And none of you sticks by the Law. Why are you seeking to kill me?"

The crowd answered, "You have a demon in you. Who's seeking to kill you?"

Jesus answered them, saying, "I did one deed and you all marvelled at it. Moses gave you circumcision (not that it's from Moses, but from your forefathers) and you circumcise a man on the Sabbath. If someone accepts circumcision on the Sabbath in order not to break the Law of Moses, are you angry with me because I made a whole man well on the Sabbath? Don't judge by superficial things, but make a proper judgement."

One striking way in which Jesus demonstrated his authority from God was in healing. The Fourth Gospel gives only three other examples of healing by Jesus (John 4, 46–54; John 9, 1–41; John 11, 38–44) in addition to the healing at the pool of Bethesda discussed above, but the other gospels are full of such stories. However, it is clear throughout that his healing ministry was important for wider reasons than simply the cure of physical problems. Some will doubt that the cases recorded are "real" cases of healing. Removal of some inner psychological barrier, inaccurate reporting or excessive credulity are all invoked to explain away such miracles. But it is clear that his ability to heal presented a real problem to the authorities. It both encouraged the people to follow Jesus and listen to his teaching and it was difficult to reconcile with the official line that he was a charlatan. Clearly the authorities did not succeed in explaining away the healing miracles and in several cases had to accept them as genuine. If this were not so, why did they find such a problem with Jesus, given their determined refusal to acknowledge that he might actually be speaking for God as he claimed?

In many of the accounts of healing, the story is designed to make an additional point which is as important as the demonstration of Jesus' link to God – the healing is done on the Sabbath to show the priority of compassion over rules, or an individual demonstrates faith, or Jesus states firmly that physical impairments are not due to sin, or Jesus demonstrates the power of love as in the raising of

Lazarus; often parallels are drawn between the curing of the physical condition, such as blindness, and the psychological blindness which Jesus can only cure with the assent of the sufferer.

John 4, 46–54

So he came again to Cana in Galilee, where he made the water into wine.

And there was a man of the royal household in Capernaum whose son was ill. This man, when he heard that Jesus had come from Judea into Galilee, went to him and asked him to come and heal his son, for he was near to death. Therefore Jesus said to him, "Unless you people see signs and wonders, you won't believe." The man said to him, "Master, come before my little son dies." Jesus said to him, "Be on your way, your son is alive."

The man believed what Jesus said to him and went off. And when he was on his way, his slaves met him and said that his son was alive. He asked them, therefore, when he began to improve. They said that the fever left him on the previous day around one o'clock. His father knew, therefore, that it happened at the time when Jesus had said to him, "Your son is alive", and he and his whole household believed. This was the second sign that Jesus performed when he came from Judea into Galilee.

John 9, 1–41, see p.80

John 11, 38–44

Jesus therefore was deeply disturbed and came to the grave. It was a cave and there was a stone lying against it. Jesus said, "Remove the stone." Martha, the sister of the dead man, said to him, "Master, by now there is a smell, for it is the fourth day." Jesus said to her, "Haven't I told you that if you believe you will see God's glory?"

So they removed the stone. Jesus turned his eyes upward and said, "Father, I thank you for listening to me. I knew that you always listen to me, but I have said this because of the surrounding crowd, so that they may believe that you sent me."

Saying this, he shouted out in a loud voice, "Lazarus, come out here." The dead man came out, with his feet and hands bound with the grave clothes and his face wrapped round with a cloth. Jesus said to them, "Free him and let him go."

And very often the healing allows an individual who has been isolated from society by the impairment (for example, a skin disease, a woman's bleeding, inability to move) to be restored to the community, as if to demonstrate that such isolation is as deadly as any physical illness. It may also be the case that Jesus healed, as much as anything, to show us that God does care about our physical well-being and would have us be as concerned about this on the local and on the global scale. In this way the healing miracles are signs of the promised new order.

Fine, you may say, Jesus was clearly a remarkable man, even perhaps a man with insight derived from a divine source. It is possible that life has a purpose that he was able to see, though you yet have to convince me of that. Why should God have created such an imperfect world, with all this suffering? If he wanted something better, why not just create it so from the start? Why this tortuous process? And I don't see how human beings can change. It seems that we would all have to experience some sort of dramatic conversion by the Holy Spirit, like St Paul, and that seems unlikely. And this purpose seems to imply that there's something we are heading for beyond this world after death and frankly that doesn't seem very realistic. How can we survive the disintegration of our physical bodies? So I need some persuasive answers about how a God who loves us could allow us to suffer, rather than doing a better job of creation, how on earth we can change our present selfish nature which has evolved over millions of years, and what happens after we die.

Why is creation imperfect?

First, then, the question of why the creator did not produce a "better" creation. Much, but not all, suffering is the result of human priorities and behaviour. And much of it would be preventable through better use of the knowledge we have, if we were prepared to use it appropriately.

It is because we are conscious beings, with the ability to be aware of the mental life of others, that we can suffer when we see others suffering and can suffer in anticipation of our own or others' suffering. The other side of the coin is that these abilities are essential to the positive side of human nature. These capacities, from which our suffering arises, are also the source of love, seeing the needs of others and rejoicing in their joys and hence essential for the changes we are advocating in human behaviour. Psychopaths lack not only the ability to understand others' suffering, but also to feel the joys of others.

The alternative to our freedom to make a mess of things would seem to be a world of robotic puppets who are pre-programmed to ensure that everything runs like clockwork and who have no emotional reactions or consciousness or aspirations. This seems somehow a worthless creation to human minds, so might not a creative God make the same judgement? Those who attempt to design Artificial Intelligences that can display some form of independent ability to learn from experience and make choices that are not simply built into them, have found that they face a similar dilemma. They have to turn their systems loose to face the demands of the environment and to make mistakes, if these systems are to adapt themselves to cope with the variety of challenges that they may face. Parents face the same problem with their children. Freedom to face challenges, make mistakes and, we hope, to learn from them, is inherent in freedom to develop and achieve and gain maturity.

Can human beings change?

How then can human beings change? Jesus promised that after he had left this world, there would still be a Helper to support our attempts to understand and follow his teaching. He several times assures the disciples that when he is no longer with them, they will be given help from the Holy Spirit. (John 14, 15–26 presents one such occasion.) This is one of the most difficult and controversial aspects of his teaching. The Spirit is referred to most commonly by the Greek word for breath, Pneuma, but the Fourth Gospel has a word of its own, Paraclete, which means Adviser, Counsellor, Teacher, Helper or Supporter. Often too this Gospel refers to "the Spirit, the Truth" or "the Spirit of truth" and in one place it combines all three terms ("I will ask the Father and he will give you another Adviser to be with you for ever, the Spirit of truth," John 14, 15). This Spirit will only be available when Jesus is no longer present (John 16, 7). (Maybe this is the real meaning of the second coming, not some remote event at the end of time.) Jesus is a human being who exemplifies the "spirit" of God in a physical body. The Spirit is non-physical and imparts information about God and further interpretation of what Jesus taught. Jesus also stated (John 4, 24) that God is Spirit. Christian theology has struggled interminably, indecisively and often bitterly in a fruitless effort to define the indefinable, and eventually produced the curious doctrine of the Trinity in an effort to agree on what could not be understood. Clearly God must exist in a different way from the physical existence which is all we can experience directly. Our notion of "Person" necessarily depends on a physical body, but we do have some notion of different personalities, even in one body, different ways of operating. If Jesus did indeed know God directly, he was attempting to depict the incomprehensible to his hearers in the simplest way he could. The use of "Spirit" aptly conveys the notion that they will be able to continue receiving

God's influence even though Jesus himself is no longer physically present to bridge the seeming gap between humanity and God.

John 14, 15–26

If you love me, you will observe my commandments. And I will ask the Father and he will give you another Adviser, so that he can stay with you for ever, the Spirit of truth, whom the world cannot comprehend because it neither sees him nor knows him. You know him because he remains by you and will be in you. I won't leave you bereft, I will come to you. In a little while the world will no longer see me, but you will see me, because I am alive and you will be alive too. On that day you will know that I am in my father and you are in me and I am in you. The one who holds my commands and observes them, he is the one who loves me. And he who loves me will be loved by my father, and I will love him and will reveal myself to him.

Judas [not Iscariot] said to him, "Master, how can it be that you will reveal yourself to us and not to the world?" Jesus answered, "If someone loves me he will observe my words, and my father will love him and we will come to him and we will stay with him. But he who does not love me will not observe my words. The word you are all hearing is not mine but comes from the Father who sent me.

"I have proclaimed these things to you while I am with you. The Adviser, the Holy Spirit, whom the Father sends in my name, he will teach you all things and will remind you of all the things which I said to you."

The Spirit is given, not to ensure our sanctity, but to continue reminding us of Jesus' challenges and to give insight into their implications for our time and place. The Spirit puts things before us like a good infant teacher and allows us space to work them out, but does not give up when we take no notice. If we expect nothing from the Spirit most of the time and just call for help when we have decided what we want, little will come of this partnership. Though the events of the first Pentecost, when the disciples spoke in tongues upon the arrival of the Spirit, have often been taken as the authentic sign of the Spirit's presence, and such speaking is regarded as a distinctive mark of true followers by the Pentecostal traditions of Christianity, Jesus' words suggest a more sedate, rational function directed at ensuring that his teaching will be developed and incorporated into human thought processes as the situation develops.

What is eternal life?

And what of eternal life? The traditional interpretation has been that Christ's death and resurrection offer eternal life to all those who believe in him. It is not clear what happens to the rest outside this magic circle, though the early Church clearly believed they would be treated as outsiders should be treated and banished somewhere unpleasant. A more appealing interpretation is that the proffered gift of the Spirit offers the possibility of taking our understanding and actions beyond the confines imposed by our current biological existence and hence growing into a form of existence in which the limitations of material bodies can eventually be put completely aside (a continuation of the evolutionary process). The body is a tool in developing toward this, not a taskmaster to be served in its own right. But we suggest this should be seen as an extension of a natural (and probably gradual) evolutionary process from matter to life to consciousness to willing co-operation. If love is the secret of living this life to the full, then surely life hereafter too must centre on love. Without love and the Spirit, human life remains fixed at the level of selfish competition, struggle, violence and eventually death and destruction.

Many may find this is a step too far. Love as an alternative principle for running the world seems a fine idea, somewhat idealistic perhaps, but nevertheless an ideal for which we can strive. It may even be possible that there are forces we do not fully understand which can support us in aiming for this ideal. We do have lesser earthly parallels where loving support from others can have amazing effects on a person's life. But that we can develop through love to a life beyond our mortal bodies, that is stretching the limits of credulity.

Once again we would point out that the certainties of science are always changing, that our understanding of matter, energy, life and so forth is slight, and that there are hints in human experience that there is more to our existence than meets the eye. We discuss in the next chapter the failure of attempts to explain human consciousness in terms of brain processes, and suggest that consciousness must be regarded as unexplained, a key "given" in our humanity. Those who recount "near death" experiences show a remarkable similarity in their accounts, even when ignorant of the related experiences of others, and "out-of-the-body" experiences have been reported which are not amenable to any simple explanation. Though it is often impossible to establish whether the experiences recounted actually occurred when the brain was clinically dead, rather than just before the loss of brain activity or during the return to consciousness, in one well-established case a woman recounted that she had experienced incidents which had occurred in the operating theatre while she was attached to instruments which demonstrated that her brain was not functioning. Of particular interest in the present context is that those who experience a near-death experience very often report an experience of profound love and awareness of others. Many of them totally change their priorities after such an event and one man, previously a tough entrepreneur, became a counsellor and reported that the richness of his new life was "like the Sistine chapel" (*The Day I Died*, BBC 2, 5 February 2003). These experiences match surprisingly closely the argument we have been pursuing. So there is much that we do not understand and to dismiss the promises of Jesus out-of-hand is to remain fixed in just that set frame of thinking from which he urges us to break out.

Just as the needs and well-being of the self form the general background to our thoughts and activities for much of the time, so, if we can move toward the new thinking that Jesus advocates, the needs and well-being of others would become the new general background, so that a conscious shift of thought from the self to others would not be constantly necessary. Such a background to our thinking would mean that we were coming much closer to the notion of being born of the Spirit, and that we were beginning to be on what might be termed the same wavelength as the God of whom Jesus speaks.

And is it so strange that such a life, no longer driven by physical needs but growing out of and nourishing these other more "spiritual" human qualities should not suddenly come to an end in death? People frequently expect to continue the knowledge of love once known in this life in a "fuller life" beyond. Jesus comes back again and again to the offer of life and equally again and again the offer is bound up with love and truth. If we are capable of evolution beyond the present state, then it could arguably bring with it the hope of clearer knowledge of truth, an ability to extend the range and depth of our love for one another across all the boundaries we normally erect and out of all that should emerge a much fuller life. All this Jesus Christ seems to propose. His resurrection endorses the promises made.

Thus we do not envisage a single piece of "magic" that grants eternal life to the believer, but rather a process of development toward a life not tied to the body. Just as proper care for our physical bodies can increase their potential and capacity for survival, so our potential for a fuller life outside physical constraints can be developed and nurtured through the exercise of love. True faith in Jesus, which is far more than passing through a few prescribed rituals, automatically entails commitment to this life of love, so in this sense it will be the key to living beyond the death of the physical body. It is not that those without this commitment are condemned in any sense, or punished, but that they will not have developed the capacity necessary for the fuller life. But, as pointed out above, we do not imply an all-or-none division between "the saved" and the rest, but rather differences in levels of development toward living beyond the body.

Chapter 6
Creation

In the previous chapter we discussed the nature of Jesus and his message, pointing out that for him his whole life, what he said and what he did, depended on his belief in a God with certain attributes. Belief in the existence of a god, though with very different attributes from those described by Jesus, presented no problem for his hearers, for the existence of gods of some sort or the Old Testament God in particular was not questioned. For our age, however, there is uncertainty over the very existence of any such being, especially among those who shape our current ways of thinking. Over the world as a whole, there is of course still widespread belief in gods of various sorts and we have discussed the inadequacies of many of the assumptions about those gods. We must now turn to the viewpoints which are widely taken as demonstrating through rational argument that any such notions are mere superstitions, the relics of old ways of thinking and ignorance about the way the universe functions. So we come now to the issues of creation, first, of the physical universe and, second of life and all that developed from that. We will argue that the course of creation shows so many uncertainties and coincidences that it is equally an act of faith to believe that science has explained everything as to believe in a creator. Both are ultimately acts of faith, and neither is a certain deduction from the facts as we know them.

The Universe

If the existence of the universe and the solar system and our planet within it is the result of a sequence of events which are totally explicable in terms of already known laws of physics and chemistry and which require no further explanation, clearly a search for a deeper meaning to human existence would be pointless. In that scenario we are but puppets of inexorable forces that will run their course whatever we do. We may have the illusion of choice but it is just that, an illusion, and our mental gropings merely seek to impose a purpose where none exists. True there is the insistent question as to how and why the chain of events began. And, an even more basic question, "Why is there (and was there) anything at all and not just nothing?" as the famous philosopher Leibniz asked. Or, as another famous philosopher, Wittgenstein, put it, it's "not how the world is, [that] is the mystical, but that it is". Frequently these questions are either assumed to be answerable ultimately in the same terms as science employs in dealing with more limited questions, though this is no more than an article of faith; or alternatively they are regarded as inadmissible, though this would seem to be simply dodging the big issues.

A further problem for mechanistic explanations is that the causal chain of events which we sketch below includes many instances of extremely unlikely occurrences, the combined probability of which occurring by chance is so small as to be barely calculable. Scientists would normally regard such low chances as strong indications that some causal factor was at work, unidentified perhaps but nevertheless exerting its effects. However, the hard-nosed scientist will argue back that, given time, even the infinitesimally improbable can occur (see, for example, Dawkins, 1989, p. 15) and the existence of the universe is one example of this truth. Because the universe is here, the argument from improbability is claimed to be inappropriate. This is rather like agreeing to play a game by the rules but asking for them to be changed as soon as the score starts mounting in the opponents' favour. We query the likelihood of so many delicately balanced steps just happening to follow one another.

Creation

There is also the question of why the original materials available were of such a kind that they could combine into the many different atoms needed for the universe we have. Could the nature of things have been different and, if so, what different universe, if any, could have emerged? Science can describe what exists around us and the sequences of change that occur. Many scientists would argue that, not only is this all that they can do, but that it is sufficient as an explanation of what is. Once we understand the sequence of events, this rules out further questions. Science deals only with the given and there is no call to go further. The question "why?" is inadmissible. But while it may be unanswerable in the terms of current science, it is certainly a question that can be raised and indeed frequently is raised. Theories about the nature of creation are plentiful, with various gods and mythological figures involved, but these perhaps reflect a long-standing human desire for some kind of meaningful beginning to the universe. The preference of many scientists for the notion of a universe coming into existence through chance rather than design has, on the other hand, much to do perhaps with the desire to assert the ability of human beings to think everything through on their own. Human beings have now, it is assumed, discovered the resources to do just that and no consideration of their possible limitations should discourage them.

The universe, it is now generally accepted, began with a Big Bang which blew apart a point of infinitely dense matter out and out into space, where it is still expanding ("out into space" is strictly incorrect as space and time do not exist except within the confines of the already expanded universe). One day this expansion may reach a limit and start shrinking back again when the force of the explosion is exhausted. But in the time between, extraordinary things have happened and go on happening. The most interesting point about the Big Bang is that, if it had been just a bit weaker, everything would have collapsed back again too quickly for the developments that followed to happen. But if the Big Bang had been just a bit stronger, everything would have flown far apart without combining into galaxies and stars and planets. So somehow, it was at just the right strength to enable galaxies, worlds and human beings to emerge. In fact, so finely tuned was the force that the argument persists as to whether expansion can go on for ever or will one day run out of steam, to be followed by contraction.

Several other things were just right too. Gravity is one of the fundamental forces in the universe, a "given" which is accepted but not explained. The force of gravity is just strong enough to make matter come together into stars and without stars like our Sun there would be no life. But if gravity were a bit stronger, stars would pull so much matter together that they would burn up too fast to support further developments. Another strange coincidence is that there was a slight imbalance in the amount of particles and antiparticles produced by the Big Bang. John Barrow (1988, p. 306) comments that this was very fortunate because otherwise,

> In the enormous densities of the early moments of the Big Bang the result would have been a catastrophic annihilation of matter and antimatter into radiation ... The average density of material in the Universe today would be more than ten billion times less than what it is, and too sparse for galaxies and stars ever to emerge.

And again, our Sun is just the right size to keep burning slowly for a long time, long enough for life to develop here on Earth.

Something else happens inside stars which is crucial to the development of life; the production of carbon. Carbon needs a very unlikely simultaneous collision of three helium nuclei. It is as if you fired three bullets into the air and got them all to collide at once. It shouldn't happen but it does and this is, we are told, because when two nuclei collide they enter into a special "resonant" state that is just right for the addition of a third helium nucleus. Even more amazing, the new combination could easily be turned into oxygen if further helium nuclei reacted with it, but they don't because the carbon combination enters into a new resonant state that is just at the wrong level for attracting further nuclei. On such fine tuning of the states of elements does our existence depend and scientific explanation consists only of inventing a label for the phenomenon! Fred Hoyle, formerly Professor of Astronomy at Cambridge, who was a strong atheist in his youth, was so impressed by this and other coincidences in the universe that he was in his later years willing to refer to, "He who fixed it".

All the elements needed for life were originally created inside the stars and trapped inside them. No life could form there but these elements managed to get out and collect where life could evolve on our Earth and perhaps elsewhere. A special sort of particle which can travel through anything, pushes these elements out of the star into space – yet one more strange fact in the story. These elements then had to gather together at a distance not too close to the Sun and not too far from it. Earth is in just the right position for life to start evolving and, of course, a whole lot more strange coincidences were needed before human beings appeared.

If the Earth were smaller it would have no atmosphere. Earth's iron core and resulting magnetic field divert the solar wind and thereby protect the atmosphere. But this core is only there because the Earth was large enough to heat up and liquidify, allowing lighter elements to come to the surface. It is also a miracle that Earth's climate remains as stable as it does. It depends on a complex interaction of water, cycling of carbon dioxide into the atmosphere through volcanoes, and absorption of this carbon dioxide by living things. Though the Sun has heated up by 26% over time, the Earth's temperature has not changed to the same extent because the presence of life maintains the stability of the climate. Furthermore, without the presence of the Moon and its pull on the Earth, the orbit of the Earth would wobble, causing huge fluctuations in temperature, which would make life virtually impossible. Many more examples of the combination of improbabilities that is necessary for the emergence of human beings have been collected and discussed by Denton (1998).

The firm conclusion which emerges from considerations such as these is that "in order for a universe to contain living observers ... the constancies of nature – or at any rate, a very large number of them – need to have values very close to those observed" (Barrow, 1994, p. 126). Denton argues that the simplest explanation is that the creation was designed to produce human beings. The universe in which we live is improbable, but we could not even exist in a more probable one. It is up to us to decide what conclusions we might draw from these considerations, but clearly the supposedly "scientific" explanation based on chance and physical/chemical laws is no more or less compelling than the conclusion that the universe is the result of design. Both are interpretations of the facts, hypotheses that are unlikely to be confirmed one way or the other by additional facts of a similar nature. For all we know there may be huge numbers of other universes where the unlikely coincidences of our own have not occurred, but there is no foreseeable way in which we could ever know this. And even if in some unforeseen way we could come to such knowledge, the question raised at the beginning of this chapter would still arise – how and why did all this begin? Of course the answers "it just did" and "God did it" both represent recourse to a "given" which refuses further explanation, and in that sense have a similar status. The postulated God, like the unexplained assertion, is no more than an escape clause from further explanation. And such a God has no further attributes relevant to human existence. To consider whether we might want to go further and say more about the nature of such a being, the implications of this being's existence for humans and relations between such a being and humanity, requires explorations and considerations of a quite different sort, which we have already examined. Here we simply argue that what we know of the evolution of the physical world certainly does not rule out the hypothesis that we are here by design rather than by chance, so our earlier discussions of the nature of God are not based on an untenable assumption.

What we are saying, in effect, is that in the end, if we do wish to make a choice, whichever choice we make is a matter of belief or faith, rather than a logical conclusion deduced from the facts. We have already pointed out that faith is present in most of our daily actions and not some childish hangover which is the preserve of religion and should be scorned by any rational being. We need always to bear in mind that our scientific models are no more than models, images of a reality we only partly understand, not the exposure of the final reality. And such theories are influenced by the context in which they develop. Evolutionary theories emphasise competition, as did the prevailing economic and social theories of the age in which they developed. Yet we can see better now that nature is an intricate web of co-operating genes, both within the organism and between organisms. Co-operation was at least as important in the evolution of life as competition, yet its role has been minimised in the theoretical accounts. We turn now to a consideration of the evolution of life.

Life

If the coming into existence of the universe is an improbable event, the emergence of life and its development into human beings with a brain that can represent these same events within their heads might be regarded as completely ridiculous. Can this extraordinary process be explained simply in terms of chance mutations and the survival of what works successfully? Are living things just complex combinations of matter packed with interacting chemical and electrical processes, in effect elaborate machines? Above all, are human beings no more than the most complex of these combinations with attributes which have emerged out of the complexity in some way we cannot currently explain, but which eventually, we can be sure, will be explicable in the same terms?

A "primeval soup" has been postulated which contained just the right mix of elements to enable life to get going, apparently just by accident (Dawkins, 1989, p. 15). But according to Francis Crick (quoted by John Maddox, 1998, p. 132) "the chances that the long polymer molecules that vitally sustain all living things could have been assembled by random processes from the chemical units of which they are made are so small as to be negligible, promoting the question whether the surface of the Earth was fertilised from elsewhere". This idea, originally proposed by Fred Hoyle, is a possibility that is increasingly touted, due to the speed at which life developed once conditions permitted it. However, this would of course simply raise the question of how life had emerged elsewhere, in some corner of the universe presumably more suited to such a development than Earth was at this point in time. Yet, as we argued above, a number of factors made the Earth particularly appropriate for the emergence of life, highly improbable though this emergence remains even in that environment. Nevertheless living things have been found everywhere on Earth, even in volcanic vents at the bottom of the ocean and at the bottom of oil wells 1500 metres deep (Maddox, 1998, p. 144). Either scientists have greatly miscalculated the probabilities or there is some other factor at work here, which led to the emergence of life on Earth.

But life did not stop with simple forms. Single cells developed into many variations and combined into larger units. The changes depended on the evolution of what Dawkins (1989, p. 15) calls "replicator molecules", which could make copies of themselves. These were the prototypes of self-replicating genes within living cells, which contain programmes of instructions for producing different forms of protein adapted to different functions of the body. The development of new genes can be attributed to chance mutations in the sequence of instructions. Very few of these mutations produce beneficial results, so most of them perish because they do not confer on the cell any advantage, but those which produce some survival advantage will increase throughout the population.

How plausible is this suggested process? Supposedly the survival of the newly mutated gene depends on its usefulness. But few genes act in isolation (Waldrop, 1994, p. 167). Important processes like extracting energy from glucose or controlling cell combinations to form particular types of tissue require several genes to co-operate. Results depend on combinations. (We pointed out above that the emphasis on competition in genetic evolution may have been in part due to the emphasis on competition in the economic and political spheres during the period when the theory developed.) As Le Fanu points out (1999, p. 309), genes act together like an orchestra. Their "meaning" depends on their context. "It is almost impossible to disentangle the contribution of one gene from that of another. A given gene will have many different effects on quite different parts of the body" (Dawkins, 1989, p. 24). Hence it is rare that changing a single gene has a simple effect (genetic engineers beware!). And even if a gene has a clearly defined physiological effect, such as loss of the ability to produce a specific protein which is needed for some bodily function, impaired function of this gene affects the whole body and thereby the survival of all the other genes. For example, damage to one known gene affects production of a specific protein present in various organs and produces the learning disability known as Fragile-X syndrome, which is characterised by a variety of intellectual deficits. But even at a lower level of the operation of specific components of the body, genes combine. Take the example of haemoglobin (Brown, 1999, p. 31). On chromosome 11 is a gene that contains instructions for producing a protein called beta haemoglobin. The instructions specify a string of 146 amino acids and twist the string into a particular shape. To produce functioning haemoglobin, two such shapes must be combined with two slightly different molecules called alpha haemoglobin, specified by a different set of genetic instructions.

So how did "useful" genes such as these survive if they needed co-operation from others to perform their function and these other genes did not yet exist? The newly evolved genes were useless on their own and should have perished. Once we accept that interactions between genes are essential for life, successful evolution becomes yet more improbable and the fact that it did occur even more astonishing. As Roger Penrose (1989, pp. 537–538) writes, "To my way of thinking, there is still something mysterious about evolution, with its apparent 'groping' towards some future purpose. Things at least seem to organise themselves somewhat better than they 'ought' to, just on the basis of blind-chance evolution and natural selection."

Consciousness

The development from living things to a living thing that can reflect on its own existence was one more step in the evolutionary process. We come to the mystery of human consciousness. First, we need to decide what we mean by consciousness, since the word has several different aspects and meanings. Then we need to ask why this ability has developed. This question is clearly linked to questions about the origin and source of consciousness; can it be explained in terms of some aspect of brain function?

We are not primarily concerned here with the distinction between being conscious (aware) of an event or not aware, most clearly exemplified in the difference between being awake and asleep (aware of very little). Individual animals show gradations of consciousness in this sense. We are concerned with the fact, known to each one of us (other than very young infants and those with some forms of brain damage) that we have experiences that imply that there is an "I" to register them. We can reflect on our experience and we can know that there is a continuity in the experiences of this "I". John McCrone (1999, p. 299) writes,

> Broadly speaking, the self-awareness of human beings has two elements: the first is the act of being self-aware, of adopting a retrospective stance to each moment and taking notice of the fact that things are happening in our heads; the second is having a knowledge of being a self. We learn to form a detached view of ourselves as a mental being. Neither of these is natural to the brain ... the brain has no evolutionary use for contemplation. It exists for the representation of reactions rather than sensations.

We also have the experience of being able to will actions, though there is huge controversy on whether this may be merely an illusion matter, which react in adaptive ways to events in order to preserve themselves, there is no obvious reason why any of this life needs to be experienced rather than merely happening in the same way as a car engine or TV set moves through a series of states of activity. If the brain is just a system for controlling the flow of information, and modifying the neural switches to ensure more efficient reactions in future, why add this extra function? Even though much that happens in the brain does not enter consciousness, it is enough for this argument that some does.

And we might add that human brains spend a lot of time and effort contemplating things which are completely peripheral to survival, but which are most distinctively human, like the meaning and purpose of their existence, religious issues and the arts.

What, then is the purpose of this awareness of ourselves and the experiences which accompany our waking (and sometimes our sleeping) life? Why did it evolve? Some have argued that it is precisely the ability to contemplate past and future that is the critical function of consciousness and explains its evolutionary advantage. The ability not to respond to an input with the strongest associated response, but to compare and evaluate possibilities both enlarges the range of possible behaviour and gives rise to the sense of an I who chooses rather than being pushed and pulled by external events. Such abilities are, in principle, explicable in terms of the further development of simpler processes such as memory, inhibition, attention and so forth, of which we already have some degree of understanding, and hence the more complex abilities could arise from increased complexity in the organisation of the brain. And, of course, simpler forms of such possible component processes are present in other animals. While this is a plausible description of key aspects of our internal experience, as an explanation it merely pushes the question one step further back. Such comparisons and evaluations could equally proceed without consciousness just like their lower constituents.

We suggest another possibility. We pointed out earlier that much human suffering occurs because we are conscious beings and thereby have the ability to look back and forwards and to empathise with others and understand tragedy. Because we are conscious we can also foresee (in part at least) the consequences of our own actions on others and the pleasure or pain that may be caused by these actions. So not only can consciousness contribute to our well-being because we can look back and plan ahead more effectively, but it enables us, potentially at least, to choose our actions for the good (or harm) of others. Hence such choice depends on being able to represent the internal life of the other in parallel with our own. This surely is only possible by the experiencing we call consciousness.

Unfortunately human ability to foresee the consequences of actions seems to have had little effect on much behaviour to date, suggesting that it is limited or overridden by other considerations. But since it also enables us to reflect on our experiences and query their significance, so that we may in turn better understand what we are doing or failing to do towards the well-being of others, then it is arguably of immense importance for any ultimate shift in our thinking toward a total regard for all humankind. Perhaps appreciation of this truth will stimulate a real step forward toward understanding this ability and using it for the purpose for which it was intended. Such an appreciation would have to be part of the new way of looking at life that Jesus urged upon his listeners.

Here then is one plausible suggestion for the key function of consciousness, the reason for its emergence, and a link with the claim that creation has a purpose. We suggest that consciousness is essential for the change of thinking which can produce the next step in evolution.

Such a proposal will of course cut little ice with those who claim that consciousness is simply an "emergent property" which develops once the brain reaches a certain level of complexity, and that the sense of self and free choice are merely illusions. We may note in passing that in making such statements they are asserting their own ability to choose, for if the assertion were determined in the same way as they claim all events are determined, it has no more validity than the statements of those who advocate the opposite view. The whole notion of truth becomes an illusion too, on this view. Both assertions are either equally the result of the relentless flow of cause and effect which has continued over all time, or both are freely chosen opinions based on contemplation of the world, either of which may or may not approach the truth. And if the latter is the case, then not everything is determined.

Returning to the evolution of consciousness, some elementary form of consciousness is now commonly ascribed to animals partly on the grounds of genetic identities (chimpanzees share 98% of human genes) and partly on the grounds of simple experimental investigations (such as demonstrations of apes solving problems while "doing nothing" or attempting to wipe a mark off their faces when they see themselves in a mirror). However, so far as we can tell, despite only small genetic differences (and they are surprisingly small, even when we compare humans and flatworms!), there are vast qualitative differences between humans and even our closest biological relatives. Science has no idea what produces these differences. Clearly the whole which emerges out of the addition of a few extra genes is much greater than the sum of the parts. Even the great apes, we can safely say, do not reflect upon the origins of the universe, life and death and their own nature. The questions addressed so far in this book arise only because humans have the capacity and mental tools to consider them. (Indeed, in a sense, the universe itself is a creation in the minds of human beings.) Is this merely a small difference on a continuum due to just another small genetic change or does it imply something more? If it is due simply to another small genetic change, "a lucky throw in the cosmic lottery", as the philosopher, John Gray, would have it (Gray, 2002, p. 30), does this not suggest that we have little real understanding of the combined potential of the genes and of what may yet develop? Alternatively, there is more to consciousness than the mechanistic results of the actions of the genes.

Daniel Dennett, for example (*The Psychologist*, October 2001), argues that consciousness is simply the ability of higher centres in the brain to represent lower processes. This view is an article of faith rather than a convincing proof, amounting to no more than pointing at how things are and saying that's how it must have happened. Similarly John Searle (1999, p. 53) says that consciousness is simply one more function of biological systems, like digestion, ignoring the fact that the latter is a process, the purpose and functioning of which we understand, and the former, at least in one sense, is a quality resulting from some process, the function of which is not apparent in the same terms and the constituent processes of which are a mystery. Removing the appropriate organs will destroy the ability to digest. In the case of consciousness, however, while damage to the hippocampus destroys the memory system needed to create continuity of experience and thus impairs one aspect of consciousness, and damage to the frontal lobes impairs other features of consciousness such as planning, in neither case does the individual cease to have a sense of identity.

Even many scientists find it hard to swallow the argument that consciousness springs suddenly from a sufficiently complex brain. Penrose (1989, p. 579) writes,

> Consciousness seems to me to be such an important phenomenon that I simply cannot believe that it is something just "accidentally" conjured up by a complicated computation. It is the phenomenon whereby the universe's very existence is made known. One can argue that a universe governed by laws that do not allow consciousness is no universe at all.

And what gives rise to the certainty that "I" have a continuity, that I am the same I throughout my life? It has been argued that this sense of the unity of experience at any one time and across time is illusory. For example, changes in a scene between eye movements are not noticed so the sense that the whole scene is experienced is mistaken. Rather, it is argued, the brain consists of many separate systems each going its own way, more like a collective than a hierarchy, a "bundle" rather than a self. But these ideas do not solve the problem that there is a sense of unity that needs explaining. What is responsible for it? What is it that registers these different inputs and seems to combine them over space and time? If it is an illusion, what produces it and why did it ever evolve? Nothing in current psychological theory can explain this continuity, for the contents of current awareness (so-called Working Memory) are constantly changing as one computation follows another (rather as the physical cells in our bodies are continually replaced by new ones, so continuity cannot depend on strict physical identity). While overlap in the changing contents of Working Memory may occur over time, it need not, and nothing remains permanently in the store. Yet at each moment the idea of which I am currently conscious presupposes a myriad of other things I know and which are necessary for my current awareness to have meaning. As I write, I "know" about computer keyboards, something about how computers work, about hands, books, publishers, readers, paper, trees, my lectures as a student, my school, home ... In a sense each conscious idea I have depends on all of my memory, and all those different pieces of knowledge contribute to it. Yet individual memories are not localised in any specific area of the brain, but distributed all over it and different memories are distributed in different parts. So how do I know that I know more than the current contents of my awareness and that I am the same person as knows those other things? And when I wake up, how do I know that I am the same person as I was yesterday? Putting it another way, how does Working Memory know that there is a huge stock of memories drawn from continuous experience residing in Long Term Memory? As pointed out above, damage to memory does not eliminate personal awareness, further reinforcing the argument that memory is not critical for this. A man may remember nothing that happens to him in the years after an event which caused a certain type of damage to the brain, yet he still regards himself as a person.

Something outside this shifting state of activity is needed to provide the basis for a self. One might argue more plausibly that ability to weigh, compare and choose is a consequence of being a conscious being, rather than the cause. So we could take consciousness as a "given", rather like the original matter of the universe, and explain other phenomena on this basis. The phenomenon of consciousness would therefore remain unexplained, as one physical determinist admits (Pinker, 1999, pp. 561 ff). Pinker claims to "solve" the problem by suggesting that our brains are incapable of solving some types of problem and this is one of them. He does not say that we possess insufficient knowledge at present, but can hope to solve it later, but rather that it lies outside our frame of thinking. Nor is he arguing that our brains invent problems which do not really exist, but rather that they discover problems which exist but which they cannot solve. So there is a problem, he admits, but there is no solution apparent based on the assumptions of mechanistic operations in the brain. This is very close to admitting that human beings are not, after all, just complex machines.

Despite what some scientists claim, therefore, there seems to be very little progress toward assimilating the experience of being a conscious person within the conventional framework of neural and cognitive investigation. This framework seems incapable of explaining why consciousness evolved, how it could be produced from the brain as currently understood, and the experience of a conscious and continuous self. An unbridgeable gap survives between the facts and attempts to reduce them to physical causes and there is something different about human beings compared with even their closest biological relatives. We have argued in the preceding chapters why this might be and what the implications are for the future of humanity.

In conclusion, this chapter has examined briefly theories that claim that the creation of the universe, the origin and evolution of life forms and the development of human consciousness are all completely explicable in terms of physical processes which science understands. We have attempted to show that the delicate timing on which many of these developments depended, the remote possibility of others occurring solely by chance and the unsatisfactory nature of many of the explanations suggest that such claims are acts of faith no less than the hypothesis of a creator with a purpose. Hence we suggest that the arguments we have developed in the preceding chapters about the nature and purpose of such a creator are based upon a presupposition which needs to be considered with an open mind. In our final chapter, we look at some of the ways in which human attitudes to religion must change if this open mind is to be achieved.

Chapter 7
Coming to the End of the Religious Set-up

It is vital that the preceding chapters are not seen as one more attempt to interpret the life and teaching of Jesus as the plan for a new formalised religion. Despite what happened historically, we have tried to show that the whole tenor of the record we have suggests that he had no intention to set up a new religious system, and regarded the formal system of religion of his time and place as an obstacle to coming to know God's purpose for humanity. Some will argue that, as he apparently attended the synagogue regularly, he respected the organised religion of his time. However, on at least some of these occasions he caused offence through ignoring the accepted rules by healing the sick and we have no accounts of his precise views on this point, but a good deal of evidence suggests that he had no great regard for what this organised religion had become. Since we believe that religious systems inevitably tend to develop the characteristics to which Jesus objected, there is no reason to suppose that he wished to encourage a further development with the same characteristics.

In our time the complexity of the world has become better known and there is an urgent need to see things from a global perspective, creatively and not merely with exploitation of one kind or another in mind. Hence religions that divide and set one group against another and make claims to possess the ultimate truth can now be a serious obstacle to the real needs of the world. Perhaps this was a necessary stage in our development, but along the way the divisive effects of one religion competing with another have played a strange and now, it seems, regrettable, role.

The Jews did not respond, except in limited numbers, to the preaching of the Christians. A Gospel that could be preached to the Gentiles became a religion for Gentiles. Jesus was expected to return and bring all things to a final climax. He did not; it was not yet "the last day". Mohammed claimed another vision that owed something to the Old Testament and included a nod, as it were, in Jesus' direction, but only as a prophet. The new faith was able to bind many together and can still give a feeling of belonging to those who acknowledge it all over the world. Buddhism has attracted many who despair of the monotheistic religions.

Perhaps in the course of these developments we needed to work out the significance of each chosen god-figure and also see how we could progress in learning to relate to one another. Though we may not have seen it, we have at the same time been evolving and developing our knowledge of the world and how it works and of the people in it and how they act. Have we learnt? As we have implied, God does not force us, but waits for us to make our choices in the face of what lies before us. Because we have been at a certain stage of evolution and largely dominated by self-interest, we have tended to assess all things, religions included, by their value to ourselves. Hence the problem with religions is that they cannot be reformed to meet the needs we have identified in the world, because they are so shaped by human self-interest.

And how has God fared in the course of these developments? Sometimes seen as weak and useless, sometimes as overwhelmingly autocratic and threatening, sometimes just tolerated in the hope that he will do something to further a cause, especially in times of war (when both sides, bizarrely, may pray to what they believe to be the same God), but never as Jesus showed him to be, with his endless concern for all mankind, not just for a particular group which chooses to acknowledge him in their own way for their own ends. Ultimately, religions seek to harness the power of God in the service of the individual or the religious group, and judge him on his performance in this role. Jesus, as we have seen, gives a very different notion of the real nature of divine power and its exercise. So we have to learn to see God very differently from the pictures humanity has painted so far. We also have to see ourselves very differently from our perceptions to date, if we are to come to an understanding of our proper potential role in creation.

Jesus made all this clear, but what he had to say was largely submerged in the revised focus introduced by Paul. The Christian religion in its two main facets of acknowledging Jesus as Lord (without actually knowing very much about what this involved) and acknowledging the authority of "the Church" over matters religious, was eventually carried by colonists and missionaries across the world. Yet by this time, the focal points were the forgiveness of sins, participation in the Christian community on Earth and life hereafter. The gospels were taken and taught, but also the Old Testament and the Epistles. Naturally much adaptation to suit existing religious positions also occurred. Throughout, the pressures of the present self-aware stage of human evolution dominated. Can this situation change? We believe it can if Jesus is listened to once more and his witness to God is taken seriously.

Perhaps we are at last approaching a new development in our evolution beyond the self-aware stage with all its forms of self-centredness. Can we now begin to learn the significance of an "others-aware" stage? If so, then we would also be ready to grasp better the full implications of what Jesus was talking about. We should also begin to evaluate God differently, not because he has changed, but because the thought is beginning to dawn that maybe we need to do this if we are to join with him in saving the world from our overwhelming self-centredness and greed.

Of course, if change comes, it doubtless will not happen suddenly and all at once. People will initially continue to visit places of worship for various reasons based on race, culture and tradition as much as the desire to serve or, indeed, to come to know more about God under whatever auspices he is worshipped. Wherever there is still a hope that a particular god-figure will fulfil the expectation people have in relation to him, there will be pressure to continue the old tradition. But should economic factors or changes in these expectations cause zeal to flag, or where political aims can be furthered without the need for religious support and encouragement, then changes will come. If people feel the need of a god-figure, they will cling to him (usually not her). If they can do what they want for themselves and their immediate fellows without having recourse to such a figure they will dispense with him. The steps we need to take globally are not, indeed cannot yet be, clear.

Due to our (the authors') own experience, we can see the current situation most clearly in relation to the Christian Church, which in its various branches has been prone to adjust and change here and there in an effort to reduce the trend away from it. For many elderly people the Church continues to offer a kind of shelter and a source of belonging, but will another generation follow them? We have noted the tendency of the affluent to support the Church, but how far is this just a statement of a place in society? Otherwise there is something of a void; people are too busy or too disenchanted or simply outside the church-going culture as in many inner-city areas.

Many cling to the Church as the one hope of teaching a new generation the Christian message, but in many areas no children attend. Where children do attend they are taught Bible stories which they, in due course, reject as childish. Many of the messages we have been trying to draw out of Jesus' teaching remain unappreciated and ignored. Children would, we believe, be more impressed and convinced by seeing love in action in family, local, national and international life which attempted to implement some of the Christian principles that the so-called Christian world claims to follow.

While ideally these practices of Christian faith are designed to impart the significance of Jesus' life, to stress that his promise to be with his followers is real and to nurture the experience of the Holy Spirit within, in practice they tend to become formulaic. Assurance of forgiveness is delivered week by week without undue emphasis on the corollary that we cannot feel or understand forgiveness for ourselves without a change within us by which we can also forgive others. This would have huge implications not just on the personal plane, but for the whole government of social, political and economic life.

Coming to the End of the Religious Set-up

Even in areas where the churches are sparsely attended, there is an expectation that the church will be there for christenings, for weddings, though these grow fewer as people opt to stay as partners, and for funerals. At times of crisis, such as murder, particularly of a child, people may feel the need to go to church to attend special services and, of course, the funeral. Just as there is the expectation that the building will be there, so also there is the expectation that someone specially appointed, a man, or possibly now a woman, will be there to officiate as required. Little thought goes into the question of how these buildings can be maintained and these people provided for in their often thankless position. The churches may be large, difficult and expensive to heat and to maintain, and the clergy may be lacking in any serious incentive to become involved in the surrounding community, but, though not needed by the local people most of the time, it is felt that they should be there, just in case. It is arguable whether this is defensible on any terms, especially as the land could be made available for many creative contributions to meet human needs, such as much-needed low-cost housing in inner-city areas for essential workers in the public sector. Sufficient space could be retained for a smaller building to see out the dying days of religion before a serious shift in thinking is accomplished. If the building is regarded as too old and distinguished for such treatment (and many are not) then it could at least be opened for a much wider range of activities for the benefit of the community, or indeed to help in creating a sense of community. These objectives, so often considered to be the responsibility of the state and not the state religion, are exactly those functions which we have been arguing are at the root of what Jesus was teaching about the fundamentals of a richer life for humankind.

Occasionally we see glimpses of how buildings and personnel can be used to forward the real purpose of Jesus to show a different way, cater for real needs, change thinking, but so many religious buildings are nothing but tombs for dying religion. The typical reaction of the churches when faced with a challenge to speak out is to hold a special, even a national, service, rather than to get their congregations involved in the dust and heat of the crisis.

Yet there is still the question that Jesus was asked and which is still often raised at a time of change, "What shall we do?" Given the primary need to switch direction of thought, it might seem appropriate to begin by simply allowing the notion of God-in-Christ to have ready entry into our minds. Then we could look at situations and, indeed, at people at every level of our acquaintance with the wish to gain understanding as to how we might appropriately react to them, rather than according to the usual perspective of our own sight and the way we deem them to affect us. God sees what we cannot see ourselves and is invariably able to respond if we are ready to listen, maybe just in the odd moment here or there rather than through any formalised occasion of prayer. In this way, perception of the truth can grow. If we are to become more "others-aware", we need to be able to listen to others, to hear and also make every effort to understand them. Too often even those who are formally committed to doing just that are rarely able to get beyond their own basic self-aware stage. Jesus had a full measure of "others-aware" capacity and is able to convey the implications through the Spirit. This is essentially not a diminishing but an enlarging experience.

Beyond that is the need to share concerns with others who care about what Jesus said and to work out what it would mean to bring his approach to bear in a situation. This could be local in significance or it could, through the Internet for example, reach wider or indeed be virtually global. There would be a need to work with others, to seek a common understanding with a willingness to change and to recognise that one's own immediate view of a situation may not represent the most appropriate guide to thought and action. We have talked of a God who has a total care for all humankind. We may lack anything approaching the capacity of his Spirit to be aware on this kind of global scale but we can make a beginning, we can ask questions, seek opinions and keep working with and on behalf of neglected people and on neglected issues. What should be avoided is a fresh network of leaders, a hierarchy of oversight and power and control of the lives of others. We should be able to contribute, achieve and then withdraw, if this is desirable, and always retain Jesus' picture of the humility that should accompany any exercise of authority.

It is, therefore, in no sense a recipe for a sudden rush of "do-gooding", primarily because the object must not be a demonstration of our own worthiness. We need instead to be learning all the time what it means to be caught up in the ongoing activity of the creative love of God. Because that is life-giving, we should find the promise of life fulfilled, though the nature of our contribution to the whole may at any given time not be what we might have expected. It would essentially be a time of change, growth and becoming. It would not be a question of asking God to be for us, but of discovering what it means to be for God-in-Christ. We have in this book tried, though inadequately, to point the way to the first steps toward this end.

References

Barrow, J.D. (1988). *The World within the World: a Journey to the Edge of Space and Time.* Oxford: Oxford University Press.

Barrow, J.D. (1994). *The Origin of the Universe.* London: Weidenfeld and Nicolson.

Barrow, J.D. (1998). *Impossibility: the Limits of Science and the Science of Limits.* Oxford: Oxford University Press.

Brown, A. (1999). *The Darwin Wars: How Stupid Genes Became Selfish Gods.* London: Simon and Schuster.

Conze, E. (1959). *Buddhist Scriptures.* Harmondsworth: Penguin.

Dawood, N.J. (1999). *The Koran* (fifth edition, revised). London: Penguin.

Dawkins, R. (1989). *The Selfish Gene.* Oxford: Oxford University Press.

Denton, M.J. (1998). *Nature's Destiny.*: Free Press

Douthwaite, R. (1999). *The Ecology of Money.* Foxhole, Devon: Green Books (for The Schumacher Society).

Fox, R.L. (1991). *The Unauthorised Version: Truth and Fiction in the Bible.* New York: Viking Penguin.

References

Geras, N. (1998). *The Contract of Mutual Indifference.* London: Verso.

George, V. and Wilding, P. (2002). *Globalization and Human Welfare.* Basingstoke: Palgrave.

Gray, J. (2002). *Straw Dogs: thoughts on humans and other animals.* London: Granta.

House, J.S., Landis, K.R. and Umberson, D. (1988). Social Relationships and Health. *Science*, 241, 540–545.

Hutton, W. (2002). *The World We're In.* London: Little, Brown.

Jenkins, D. (2000). *Market Whys and Human Wherefores: thinking again about markets, politics and people.* London: Cassell.

Le Fanu, J. (1999). *The Rise and Fall of Modern Medicine.* London: Little, Brown.

Lee-Chai, A.Y. and Bargh, J.A. (2001). *The Use and Abuse of Power: Multiple Perspectives on the Causes of Corruption.* Hove and Philadelphia: Psychology Press.

Maddox, J. (1998). *What Remains to be Discovered.* London: Macmillan.

McCrone, J. (1999). *Going Inside: A Tour round a single Moment of Consciousness.* London: Faber and Faber.

Morison, F. (1958). *Who Moved the Stone?* London: Faber and Faber.

Pinker, S. (1999). *How the Mind Works.* Harmondsworth: Penguin.

References

Penrose, R. (1989). *The Emperor's New Mind.* Oxford: Oxford University Press.

Powell, M.A. (1998). *The Jesus Debate.* Oxford: Lion.

Searle, J. (1999). *Mind, Language and Society: Philosophy in the Real World.* London: Weidenfeld and Nicolson.

Sterling, S. (2001). *Sustainable Education: Re-visioning learning and change.* Foxhole, Devon: Green Books (for The Schumacher Society).

Waldrop, M.M. (1994). *Complexity: the emerging science at the edge of order and chaos.* Harmondsworth: Penguin.

Biblical Passages Quoted

	Page
John 3, 1–12	36
John 4, 4–30	83
John 4, 46–54	109
John 5, 1–18	105
John 6; 1–15, 25–29	39
John 7, 10–24	107
John 8, 1–11	77
John 9, 1–41	80
John 13, 1–16	56
John 13, 31–35	47
John 14, 15–26	113
Luke 4, 1–13	55
Mark 10, 17–27	51
Matthew 5, 1–10	43
Matthew 6, 7–13	87

Index

Alpha course	4
Arms trade	22
Atonement	8, 95
Beatitudes	34, 42
Big bang	121, 122
Born again	36, 96
Buddhism	4, 136
Children	24, 26, 46, 48, 138
Choice	10, 30, 68, 92, 94, 118, 124, 128
Competition	6, 8, 13, 14, 21, 24, 25, 27, 30, 60, 96,115 125
Consciousness	97, 111, 115, 125-134
Co-operation	15, 32, 65, 73, 114, 125,
Creation	6, 71, 94, 111, 119,
Crime	12, 28, 29, 41,
Debt	15, 20, 21, 45, 64, 87,
Development	38, 72, 104, 116, 135
Drugs	18, 28, 58, 92
Education	25, 26, 63
Environment	16, 20, 23, 63, 67, 68
Eternal Life/	4, 84, 112,
Eternity	51
Evolution	6, 8, 9, 31, 44, 65, 72, 116, 124-127, 134
Faith	92, 95, 97, 119, 124, 134
Fall, The	97
Fourth Gospel	35, 40, 44, 54, 76, 90, 99, 100, 104, 106, 108, 112
Freedom	6, 8, 14, 36, 96, 111
Genes	10, 65, 73, 124, 126, 129
Globalisation	13, 14

Healing	2, 78, 79, 108, 110, 135
Individualism	8, 27, 63
Islam	4
Jews/Judaism	4, 86, 96, 100
Koran	4, 94
Life, development	5, 122
Love	8, 33, 47, 65, 68, 73, 76, 89, 96, 110, 114, 116, 138
Market	10, 13-17
Miracles	101, 103, 108, 110
Money	3, 13, 20, 22, 24-27, 49, 50, 52, 54, 61, 63
Paul/St Paul	35, 95, 96, 99
Power	12, 35, 54-59, 90, 102
Prayer	86, 87, 90, 138
Purpose	6, 7, 72, 73, 74, 127, 139
Religion	3, 7, 9, 33, 44, 93, 134, 135
Riches	2, 26, 43, 53,
Rituals	3, 8, 82, 85, 97, 116
Rules	4, 8, 33, 75, 76, 78, 85, 91, 94, 95, 105, 108
Salvation	7, 8, 35, 76, 95, 97
Science	2, 5, 9, 71, 101, 115, 119, 131
Second coming	100, 112
Self-interest	4, 39, 61, 76, 136
Sermon on the Mount	34, 42
Sin	78, 79, 96
Spirit/Holy Spirit	33, 36, 44, 100, 112
Suffering	5, 94, 111, 129
Trinity, The	112
Truth	4, 19, 43, 75, 90, 107, 112, 116, 130, 135
Wealth	14, 26, 48-53, 61, 62, 72
Women	3, 47, 78, 83, 86, 92, 95, 102
Worship	4, 82, 93, 137